Best wishes
& best of
luck

[signature]

Fighting to Win

Books by David J. Rogers

AGENCY AND COMPANY

Fighting to Win

to Win

Samurai Techniques
for Your Work and Life

David J. Rogers

Doubleday
NEW YORK   LONDON   TORONTO   SYDNEY   AUCKLAND

Published by Doubleday, a division of
Bantam Doubleday Dell Publishing Group, Inc.,
666 Fifth Avenue, New York, New York 10103

Doubleday and the portrayal of an anchor with a dolphin
are trademarks of Doubleday, a division of
Bantam Doubleday Dell Publishing Group, Inc.

Library of Congress Cataloging in Publication Data
Rogers, David J.
    Fighting to win.
    1. Success in business. 2. Conduct of life.
3. Martial arts. I. Title. II. Title: Samurai techniques
for your work and life.
HF5386.R544 1984   650.1
ISBN: 0-385-18938-9
Library of Congress Catalog Card Number 83-40135

6 8 9 7

BG

In memory of my sister Sharon
Just one word—courage

Contents

Contents

Fighting to Win

Introduction

Converting the Skills of the Samurai
to Modern Business and Personal Life

I recall the moment this book started to germinate. While negotiating a contract one afternoon I suddenly realized that although neither I nor the two men I was trying to strike a deal with were holding swords, we were in fact engaged in a very real form of combat. I was in a one-against-two fight. I didn't wish to destroy these men, but I did want the best deal possible for myself.

If that parallel was valid, wasn't it possible to transpose appropriate principles from the *kendo* (samurai swordsmanship) *dojo* (training hall) to this conference room on the fifty-seventh floor of a downtown skyscraper?

And of course it was.

The fit between what was occurring in that meeting and what samurai sword masters had met during their battles was exact.

What I had that my opponents across the table did not have was a whole, complete system for perceiving exactly what was going on, and a store of methods, techniques and approaches which I could draw on at will to get what I wanted.

I could see it clearly when the two men from the other firm attempted to counter my technique, *waza* (covered in Chapter 10), and to go after my spirit, *ki* (Chapter 4). I understood the way in which they were using their power and saw how to counter it with *marui*, "circular motion" (Chapter 8). I realized that they were looking for my *suki*, the gap in my defense (Chapter 9), so I employed a technique which I converted from samurai sword master Ittosai's technique (Chapter 10).

I walked out of that room that afternoon feeling elated. Not only did I have a signed contract and the terms I wanted, but I sensed that if these few samurai techniques had worked, surely there were others that would work just as well. And if there were, couldn't they be put into book form so that not only I, but many people could benefit from them? A number of other experiences soon convinced me that such a book might be a worthwhile undertaking.

A regional director of a government agency who was taking my graduate class in human resource management had become enamored of so-called Japanese management, and had implemented its methods and procedures in his organization. "It should be working," he told the class, "but it isn't. There's something wrong at the human level." He told me that what was wrong became clear to him when we went over what I now call "attaching" business management (Chapter 6). It is a managerial style very commonly found in business enterprises. Unfortunately it drives workers into the most harmful and least productive of all conditions, *ushin*, "self-consciousness." If there is one state of mind which the samurai strove to avoid and which managers and supervisors should *not* force their employees into, *ushin* is it.

Madelene is a lovely thirty-seven-year old woman who sells an expensive line of greeting cards, mugs and other novelty items to department stores and other retailers in downtown Chicago. She is friendly, articulate, intelligent, warm and likable. She is conscientious about constantly improving her selling technique, and, as you can imagine, she does very well for herself and the firm she represents . . . most of the time, at least.

As effective as she was at selling to most prospects, she was totally inept at relating to one particular kind of person. Doubtless you have run into your share of them—tough, abrasive, loud, unreasonable people. Mr. or Ms. Nasty.

"I'm frightened of this kind of person," Madelene said to me. "I'm scared to death of them. I know I shouldn't be, but I am. With other people I'm fine, but with people like that, I don't know, I kind of forget everything I know about selling. *I lose the ability to sell.* It's weird."

It might seem hard to imagine anyone more different from a fierce feudal Japanese warrior, his long sword drawn, than gentle saleswoman

Madelene, armed only with her order book.* Yet her problem—the sudden loss of ability when face to face with an opponent in battle—was one any number of samurai encountered too. They even described the frightening experience in virtually the same words that Madelene had used.

I quoted to her the eighteenth-century samurai maxim, "To defeat the enemy who comes leaping at you, your spirit must be perfectly poised." Now, any samurai would *feel* the truth of that maxim. Madelene felt it too. Her eyes shot wide open.

"That's what I want," she said emphatically. "Tell me more."

I tried to think of a book that I could recommend to Madelene, one that defined samurai fighting skills and provided guidelines for applying them to her particular situation. I encountered a problem—*no such book had been written. It didn't exist.*

The best samurai teachings had never been written down in a systematic fashion that would enable a person coming at the material from outside the samurai traditions to pick it up and apply it immediately. Samurai information that had been passed down through the centuries was obscure—and for good reason. No master fighter wanted his insights and techniques to become known by an opponent who might use them against him in battle. For this reason, what had been communicated in writing consisted mainly of mere notes, epigrams and highlights of samurai teachings, cryptic little sayings that might be useful if one had a lifetime to devote to understanding them, but which were of little value if you wanted to apply them this afternoon.

One thing practical-minded Madelene did not want was a long-winded explanation of why useful samurai information did not exist. She had a problem and she wanted to solve it—if possible right then and there. I did some fast on-the-spot converting—borrowing techniques from the samurai way of life and reworking them into practical advice that I was convinced would help Madelene win her battle with Mr. and Ms. Nasty. We discussed four specific techniques for achieving what the samurai called "the skill of making the body obey the mind." All of these techniques now appear in Chapter 7 of *Fighting to Win*.

"Got it?" I asked Madelene.

* The answer to the question I'm often asked, "Were there female samurai?" is yes. Tomoe of the Minamoto clan was a superb horsewoman, skilled with many weapons. A woman named Itagaki commanded 3,000 Taira warriors.

"Got it," she said.

There was only one direction that was ever important to the samurai, and that was forward, always forward. What he was worried about or feared most he went after first. Madelene did the same. She picked out a Mr. Nasty she had been avoiding and went to see him. An hour later, after having applied the techniques we had discussed, she stepped out onto the sidewalk thirteen hundred dollars richer, having sold him three complete displays. More important, she had experienced a taste of the samurai truth—"No matter what it is, there is nothing you cannot overcome."

Following that success in battle, Madelene began telephoning me for "more of that samurai stuff." Being friendly, she had many friends, and they began to call too—with battlefield problems ranging from getting ahead at the office to increasing their self-confidence.

While giving business seminars on marketing, sales and personal motivation, I periodically used samurai concepts, terms and anecdotes merely to illustrate a point. I discovered that the people in attendance not only permitted me these digressions but wanted more of the same.

Tony is a marketer who found the information now contained in Chapter 3 particularly relevant to his problem. He was, he told me, "a fairly smart guy living a very dumb life." As soon as he started following the samurai advice, *Mokuteki hon'i*, "Focus on your purpose," he began to perform his job better and to feel more intense, more alive.

An attorney friend of mine was down on himself because of the way a case he was handling was going. All it took for him to increase his confidence and drive was understanding "the swing of the advantage" (Chapter 10) and the concept of *kufu* (Chapter 5).

During a meeting with the management team of a client I was consulting with, I happened to let slip the term *mo chih ch'u* (Chapter 2). Heads turned and someone asked, "What the hell is that?"

I said it means going straight ahead without hesitation. To illustrate it I used examples from the way of life of the samurai and related it to a problem the organization was currently trying to solve.

A few weeks later I visited the client again. I found the term *mo chih ch'u* printed on the top manager's chalkboard. "It's our motto now," he said.

Years passed since that meeting when I had first converted a few samurai techniques to a business undertaking. The sense that there were probably other techniques that would work just as well had been validated many times over. In fact I had discovered that *all* the techniques, insights, methods, principles and precepts of samurai warfare could be used to improve my personal performance—and not only in business, but outside of it too.

And I discovered that I was not alone. There were many people besides myself who could learn to apply samurai fighting skills to win their battles, battles as varied as:

- defeating a business competitor
- being interviewed for a new job
- staying on a diet
- reaching major life goals
- improving sales performance
- making a career change
- accomplishing more in less time
- overcoming depression, nervousness and fear
- increasing concentration on tasks and responsibilities
- feeling more optimistic and ready for action
- enhancing your own productivity and morale and that of your coworkers and subordinates
- defeating self-doubt
- handling a crisis
  . . . and more.

Background on the Way of the Samurai

"The tramp of warriors sounded like a thousand convulsions of the earth." "The shouts of warriors, the whistling of arrows, the thunder of the feet of foot soldiers and the hooves of chargers did not cease."

According to historical chronicles, that was the sound of Japan during much of the five hundred years from 1100 to 1600, a period whose essence can be captured in the single Japanese word *arasoi,* "strife."

It was a period of almost continual warfare between powerful clans *(uji)* and warrior families *(buke);* a time of desperate marches, pitched battles and long campaigns. It was an era which saw the roads frequently clogged with columns of troops, at times stretching miles in length—the

generals *(taisho)* and captains *(sho)* and behind them the mounted and
walking warriors. Among them were the archers, masters of the longbow;
and the swordsmen whose long-sword even today is considered the finest
fighting blade ever produced by man. With them were the spearmen,
the specialists in the halberd, and the experts in the many other weapons
of war. These were the most complete fighters ever to walk the earth, the
supreme warriors, the stern, quiet men who in years to come would be
known by the one word which has become synonymous with martial
expertness—samurai.

Before the sword became so closely identified with the samurai, the
bow was his principal weapon. The most renowned archers belonged to
the immensely powerful Minamoto clan. It was said that Yoshiie of the
Minamoto (1041–1108) "shot arrows from horseback like a god . . .
He galloped like the wind." Tametomo† Minamoto was such a strong
archer that, attacked by two men in battle and finding himself with but
one arrow remaining, he shot it completely through the first man and
into the second.

To dissuade the Japanese warrior families from military incursions into
their country, Korean emissaries brought one of their famous iron war
shields to the court of Japanese Emperor Nintoku. A samurai bowman
named Tatebito respectfully asked if he might test the invincible shield.
He pierced it with his first arrow.

Power is important, but accuracy matters too. A valuable bird belong-
ing to the shogun Yoritsune escaped from its cage. A bowman quickly
fired an arrow which gently grazed the bird, bringing it fluttering to
earth without even one damaged feather.

Mongol invaders who twice returned home after being repelled by
armies of samurai recited tales of the wonderful warriors who "struck like
bolts of lightning." A Chinese historian who witnessed a battle recorded
that the samurai brandished their swords with such miraculous speed
that all that could be seen was a "blur of white steel."

The samurai were members of the Japanese professional warrior class,
whose history spanned the thousand years between the ninth and nineteenth century and which ruled Japan during much of that time.

Among the most renowned warriors were those who fought in the

† In *Fighting to Win,* Japanese names are given in their Western form—first name first,
then the family name.

service of the illustrious families of Japanese history, including the Fujiwara, Taira, Minamoto, Hojo, Ashikaga and Tokugawa.

Of the samurai generals, five stood above the rest. Masashige Kusunoki was the most revered samurai in Japanese history, a national hero whose name even today is synonymous with unswerving loyalty and bravery. Nobunaga Oda was a sixteenth-century samurai whose motto was "all the country under military control." He used his samurai forces to unify Japan militarily. Yoshitsune Minamoto was a brilliant twelfth-century general and master swordsman whose tactic of surprise attack helped to defeat the forces of the powerful Taira clan. Yoshitsune's retainer, Benkei, is renowned for his skill not with the sword or the bow but with the *naginata*, the curved blade on a pole, or halberd, which was popular among many samurai of the time. So confident was Benkei of his skill that he wrote a battlefield lament ending,

"Oh how I long
For a foe worthy of my hand."

The greatest rags-to-riches story in the annals of Japanese history is that of Hideyoshi Toyotomi, a peasant who became a samurai under Nobunaga, eventually commanded an army of two hundred thousand men and became the beneficent ruler of Japan in 1582. The crafty Ieyasu Tokugawa (Toranaga in the novel *Shogun)* was the fifth great samurai general. Ieyasu was a ruthless warrior whose decisive victory in 1600 at the battle of Sekigahara, in which two hundred and thirty thousand men crossed swords, put a permanent end to the large-scale warring among the clans.

The lowest-ranking member of the samurai class was the *ashigaru*, or "foot soldier." Like all samurai, the *ashigaru* was entitled to wear the *daisho*, or "two swords"—the long sword and the short sword—but he was denied many of the privileges of the higher-ranking and more skilled samurai—the *bushi*.

When we think of samurai, it is the *bushi* we have in mind—the elite fighters who devoted themselves to refining warfare to its highest level, the level of art. Of the *bushi*, the most highly developed warriors, the elite of the elite, were the *meijin*, the masters.

The role of the samurai warrior was to fight—with supreme self-confidence, courage, bravery and superb skill with weapons. He pledged himself to the service of a warrior chieftain *(bushi no toryo)* or lord, *daimyo*, who held power in his local province. Since the Japanese extended families of feudal times tended to be located together in the same geographical area, the local chieftain was likely to be related to the *bushi* by blood or marriage, although this was not always the case.

The bonds of allegiance between the *bushi* and his lord were to be lifelong. These bonds were held together by mutual respect and were cemented by a demanding code of personal behavior which became known as *bushido*. For centuries, *bushido* was a set of unwritten rules of conduct impressed on the samurai in his training. It was put into writing by Soko Yamaga (1622–85), a samurai teacher of the military arts and a scholar as well, in his essay "Shido."

In addition to Yamaga's essay, another famous expression of *bushido* is *Hagakure*, a book that is cited in *Fighting to Win*. *Hagakure* literally means "hidden in leaves," denoting the samurai ethic of modesty, of not blowing your own horn. Written between 1710 and 1716 by Tsunetomo Yamamoto, a retired samurai of the Nabeshima clan, *Hagakure* is a compilation of the thoughts and observations of a devout *bushi*.

The principle of duty *(giri)* was the cornerstone of *bushido*. The word "duty" evoked powerful motives in the samurai, just as it does in the Japanese of today. For the samurai, duty was an obligation that had to be met, even if it was unpleasant or painful or if it brought certain death.

Self-control was an important feature of *bushido*. The samurai's body, mind, emotions and spirit were to be under his control.

Commitment to immediate action, action carried out right now, without waiting or hesitating, formed another basis of *bushido*.

The samurai lived in a society of deviousness and intrigue, in which cheating was rampant. *Bushido* was to keep the *bushi* above such treachery. It was said, "A *bushi* has no second word," and "A *bushi* never lies." Because of their honesty, samurai were often specially selected by merchants and landowners as couriers, to carry large sums of money.

Bushido also emphasized the need for constant self-improvement. For the samurai to rest on his laurels and to continue without correcting errors and mistakes was incompatible with *bushido*.

As a part of this urge to improve, the samurai borrowed whatever he could find of value—weapons, techniques, knowledge—wherever he could find them. When he discovered a useful insight in a Chinese or Indian Buddhist classic, he incorporated it into his life. When he was beaten by an opponent he treated his defeat as an indication that the victor had something to teach him. In 1543, when two Portuguese sailors showed Lord Tokitaka the first firearm *(teppo)* any Japanese had ever seen, Tokitaka thought it was "the wonder of wonders." Typical of the samurai and the Japanese, his initial reaction of awe was followed by the request to be taught.

Through an interpreter, Tokitaka said to the sailors, "Incapable though I am, I should like to learn about it." The appellation "copycat nation" that has been applied to Japan is a disparaging way of describing this admirable trait of pragmatic openness to new learning and fresh approaches.

The ideal samurai *bushi* was a well-rounded individual—a man of war who was also a man of learning. *Bushi* were anything but simpleminded toughs. On the contrary, they were well-educated men who belonged to the highest class of Japanese society, the cultured elite who contributed directly to the advancement of the fine arts of theater, poetry, calligraphy and painting. The slogan *bunbu ryodo,* the "united ways of the pen and sword," refers to the samurai goal of developing martial *and* literary abilities.

Foreign Influences

The influence of China is apparent in every sphere of Japanese life, including the "Way" of the samurai. Look closely at Japan's philosophies of life, religions, institutions of government and learning, values, military arts and even language, and there you will find unmistakable traces of the Chinese culture.

Many of the weapons used by the samurai were modifications of older Chinese weapons. Principles of force and mental concentration of ancient Chinese martial arts such as *tai chi* and other combat forms from the Chinese *Kung Fu‡* tradition found their way into *budo,* the Way of the samurai.

The vocabulary of the samurai, like that of Japanese generally, contained a number of Chinese terms that had no precise Japanese equivalent. *Mo chih ch'u,* which is used in Chapter 2 of *Fighting to Win,* is

‡ *Kung Fu* is not a style of unarmed combat but a generic term that applies to all Chinese martial arts.

one such term. The word *kendo*, the Way of the sword, is a Chinese word. The word "samurai" itself is the Japanese pronunciation of a Chinese word.

Among the first books brought to Japan from China by Kukai (774–835) were treatises on military strategy and tactics, some of which dated back to 500 B.C. These texts were devotedly studied by the samurai, and their principles and precepts were incorporated into *budo*. A particular favorite was the Chinese general Sun Tzu, called Sonshi by the Japanese. His words echo through the written works of Musashi, the *Hagakure* of samurai Tsunetomo Yamamoto, the *Tengugeijutsuron* of Shissai and other samurai classics cited in *Fighting to Win*.

Chinese Confucianism and Taoism had a strong influence on *budo* and on Japanese culture generally. Buddhism, even today the dominant religion of Japan, reached Japan from India by way of China. Direct and indirect references to famous Indian Buddhist texts, stories and concepts are quite apparent in the traditions of the samurai Way.

Another powerful influence on *budo* was Zen, the Japanese form of Chinese Buddhism (called Ch'an). The spirit of Zen permeates the samurai Way. Zen precepts and attitudes, and even its stories, were freely appropriated and reworked by *ryu*, warrior schools, emerging from this process in samurai trappings.

The warrior class was the first segment of Japanese society to embrace Zen. From the twelfth-century Kamakura era onward, Zen became known as the religion of the samurai.* Its influence on the samurai class reached its zenith during the shogunate regency of the Hojo family (1205–1333).

It was quite common for shoguns, generals and *daimyo* to count Zen monks among their closest advisors and for Zen masters to be *kengo* ("expert swordsmen"). Takuan Soho (1573–1645), who is mentioned in this book, was both a revered Zen abbot and a skilled swordsman who taught both disciplines to samurai of the Tokugawa shogunate.

Westerners often express difficulty in reconciling Zen, a philosophy of peace and compassion, with the samurai Way of war. What explains the fit between these two apparently different approaches to life?

Zen is many things—a religion, a philosophy, a life-style. It is also a psychology, a psychology of action, grounded on decisiveness, spontane-

---

* There were in fact Christian samurai, but they, too, doubtless embraced Zen.

ity, strength of will, adaptability, courage and bravery. It was this psychological aspect of Zen which appealed most to the samurai; for to rush forward to face the enemy even if only death awaited him, he needed what Zen taught—to act without hanging back, without reservations and with total commitment.

Budo

When he was not in battle the samurai developed his fighting skills through rigorous and constant training in his "Way."

The Japanese "do" (pronounced "dough"), means "way," short for "way of life" or "life path." That a discipline is a way is indicated by the do suffix at the end of a word. Thus kendo (ken, sword; do, way) means "sword Way," or Way of the sword.

Bu (warrior) do (Way), refers to the attitudes, behavior and life-style of the samurai. Budo is comprised of a number of other Ways, other kakuto bugei, "fighting techniques." While each samurai usually specialized in the use of one or two weapons, he was expected to be familiar with the fundamentals of the others, just as a corporate manager has a particular expertise in industrial relations but is aware of at least the basic principles of financial management, marketing, production, public relations, etc.

The samurai Ways best known in the West are swordsmanship (kendo) and archery (kyudo), the big two of samurai warfare. Lesser known to most Westerners are spearsmanship (sodo), sword-drawing (iaido), halberd fighting (naginatado), and the use of the war fan (tessendo), the truncheon (juttedo), and the staff (bodo) and stick (jodo). Since he often rode a charger into battle, the samurai bushi was also to have mastered bado, horsemanship.

Although the respect paid to many of the lesser-known Ways pales in comparison with that given to samurai swordsmanship, still the skills of all these specialists were notable. "Sword saint" Musashi Miyamoto (1584–1645), author of Go Rin No Sho, A Book of Five Rings, was dealt a defeat by Gonnosuke Muso, master of jodo, the Way of the stick. Since Musashi had once beaten Muso and spared him, Muso reciprocated, permitting the famed swordsman to escape with his life.

By the eleventh century, swordsmanship had eclipsed archery as the principal art of the samurai, and a cult of the sword had developed. The *ken,* or sword, was invested with mystical attributes which the samurai was to draw out from it through his skills and the rightness of his motives. The samurai considered the sword not only his weapon but his very soul, a tangible extension of his innermost being. To use the *ken* improperly was to stain the honor of the samurai and the sword.

In the centuries that followed, many great swordsmen emerged to contribute new techniques and approaches to the tradition of the "sword Way." Often these men opened schools *(ryu)* to transmit their innovations to students. Some of these masters recorded their advice on scrolls. *Meijin* (masters) of the other Ways often did the same in transmitting their teachings.

Rarely did these scrolls pass on technical information alone. Ordinarily they were concerned at least as much with the master's philosophy of combat and his insights into the psychology of the warrior.

It is not surprising that so much emphasis is placed on psychology in all the Ways of *budo,* the warrior Way. Warriors were ordinary men who through hard training were expected to become capable of extraordinary feats of courage—something that was impossible unless they were able to overcome the fears, hesitations, doubts and second thoughts that plague anyone going into battle.

It is important to note that the learnings acquired by devoting oneself to one Way apply to the other Ways and to life generally. There is a famous story of a cowardly samurai who learned the meaning of courage by observing the calm composure with which a businessman handled the ups and downs of the marketplace.

In *kyudo,* the Way of the bow, no quiver is worn and the archer fires just one arrow. From this the archer is to learn *daido,* a "principle that operates in all things." The archer is to come to value his life more fully, for each arrow is like the totality of his life. You have but one life; thus you shoot but one arrow. *Fighting to Win* follows the *daido* tradition by relating the Way of the samurai to the Ways of business and personal life. This book follows the adage "The Way is your daily life."

Whatever his combat specialty, the master samurai was to be fully prepared for any eventuality. No matter what his circumstances in battle were, he was to have options open to him. For this reason he developed skills in unusual weapons arts. Just one was *uchi-ne,* the art of throwing arrows in the event his bow was broken or unavailable. Another was stone-throwing.

In addition, the *bushi* developed skills in weaponless, unarmed fighting styles. *Judo*, the Way of *ju*, flexible adaptation, is the best known of these hand-to-hand combat techniques. It is this Way which forms the relationship between the Way of the samurai and today's martial arts of *aikido* and *karate* (short for Okinawan *karate-do)* and the arts spawned by them. Techniques of grappling with and throwing an opponent had long been a part of samurai swordsmanship. In addition, the samurai was likely to use *judo* when he found himself in battle without access to a weapon or to defeat a person of lower social rank who was prohibited from carrying a weapon.

Samurai Training

The main feature of samurai training was that it treated the warrior holistically—as a whole person. It recognized that when one goes into battle his skill with the sword or any other weapon is inseparable from what he is experiencing subjectively, inside his mind and body. If there is fear, worry or self-doubt, the fighter's performance will be directly and inevitably affected. This is something my friend, the saleswoman Madelene, discovered for herself—namely, that she lost her ability to sell when she was up against a Mr. or Ms. Nasty.

And if the warrior is terrified, he may never even set foot on the battlefield at all, but might well run away—as do those individuals today who let opportunity slip by because they are too scared to try. Your attitudes—toward the battle, and yourself, and your chances of coming out victorious—*directly* and powerfully affect your outward performance.

From this sensible observation came the emphasis of samurai training on developing the warrior on both levels, outer and inner—holistically, as the whole person he was.

Outer development was concerned with improving the warrior's skill with weapons—the sword, halberd, bow, etc. Any skill that's visible to the eye is "outer." The salespeople whose adeptness you can actually see demonstrated in their skillful opening presentation, probing, handling of resistance and closing, have their outer, visible skills down pat. And you've got your outer skills in good order if someone can look at you performing your job and think, "This person knows exactly what he/she is doing."

Traditional business training and education—the kind received at schools and seminars—is what the samurai would call outer training in technique. It's the type that's designed, for example, to teach accountants the observable skills of cost accounting, or to teach marketers the specific skills of defining promising market segments for a product, or to instruct would-be typists in how to type. This kind of training and education focuses on the development of some outwardly observable set of skills whose acquisition can be measured objectively. In the West, when we think of training, this is the type we are thinking of.

Inner development. If you were forced to make a choice between possessing great technical business ability or an unconquerable spirit, which would you choose?

Neither the samurai nor the Japanese businessman of today would have any problem deciding. Without hesitating he would choose spirit, the fire inside. The eighteenth-century *Tengugeijutsuron* of Shissai is a discourse for samurai which contains *not one* technical direction. Why? Because, like all samurai, Shissai believed that in any battle the *person*, not the technique or the weapon, was the most important factor. The master swordsman Musashi wrote that with training a warrior should be able to beat ten men with his spirit alone. The person first, technique second: that is the emphasis of the samurai Way.

Even today in Japan the subjective side of the person is considered of far greater importance to performance than technical skill. Whatever the field—business, politics or the arts—the inner dimensions of personality, such as courage, will, commitment, intestinal fortitude—in short, the person's spirit—are considered primary: the person first, technique second.

"Your sword and your spirit must be united"; "Behind technique is the spirit"; "The warrior grows from within": these are just a few of the myriad references to the immense importance in battle of what you are as a person—your subjective self. Percentages are even given: "Zen seven, *ken* three" is a samurai saying that you hear in a martial arts *dojo* (training hall) even today. It means that technical ability with the sword *(ken)* or any other weapon (take a modern business weapon, the computer, for example), is only 30 percent responsible for your success or failure.

The 70 percent factor (the Zen of the saying) in any battle—crossing swords in *kendo*, or selling a product, or solving a problem—is inside you. Inner training is devoted to cultivating that inner power.

Can a person be trained to overcome fear? Is courage learnable? Can someone acquire self-confidence and boldness in action? Is it possible for someone to pick up the ability to leap forward against even the most formidable of foes?

The answer to such questions is found in the inner samurai training. And it is always *yes*.

The End of the Era of the Samurai

In 1603 the powerful general Ieyasu Tokugawa installed himself as shogun, the military ruler of all Japan. For the more than two and a half centuries of rule by the Tokugawa line of military dictators, peace would prevail. Warriors without a war, the Tokugawa samurai often became the administrators of the estates of their lords or settled into the life of a *ronin*.

Ronin, or "wave men," were samurai who were no longer in the employ of a lord. Without attachments, drifting like waves, *ronin* sought other types of employment, became bodyguards to the wealthy or, like the *ronin* swordsman Musashi, journeyed across Japan maintaining the Way of the warrior in bouts with other samurai.

The Meiji Restoration of 1868 put an end to the *bakufu*, the arrangement whereby the emperor was the spiritual figurehead of Japan but the military shoguns actually ruled. The samurai class was abolished and a law was passed making it illegal to carry swords. The priority of the time was peace, not war. It was clear that the feudal governments of the past had left Japan an industrially backward society in comparison with the powerful countries of the West. The rallying cry of the time became *gaikoku to kata wo naraberu*, "abreast of Western nations."

Since they were often among the best-educated people in Japan, samurai generally had little difficulty turning their considerable talents to nonmilitary pursuits such as business, banking, civil service, politics and education.

Yet the traditions of *budo* did not die out. Even as the official status of the samurai as the elite of Japanese society ended, the values and attitudes which these warriors advanced remained an essential part of Japanese life. As a well-known Japanese professor wrote, "Scratch a Japanese of the most advanced ideas, and he will show a samurai." Even today, much of what is called Japanese business management is not completely understandable to a person who lacks familiarity with *budo*, the Way of the samurai, and *bushido*, the samurai code.

The Design of This Book

Fighting to Win is a practical handbook of *musha-shugyo*, "training in warriorship." It describes a systematic, step-by-step approach to effectiveness at work and in your personal life. It is also designed to be used by businesses wishing to improve their fighting skills.

Each chapter focuses on one key element of *budo*, the Way of the samurai, which you can readily utilize in your daily life. The format of each chapter follows a pattern:

• An essential fighting skill of the samurai is identified and described.

• Illustrative anecdotes and examples are presented. They are drawn from two areas, the samurai tradition and modern business and life. You are shown how the skill was applied by the *bushi* (the elite samurai) and you also see how the very same skill works just as effectively today.

• Throughout, you are provided with a new vocabulary, a fresh terminology for bringing about positive changes in your life. When Japanese words are used, they are clearly defined. They are not difficult to remember.

• Practical strategies, tips, recommendations and suggestions are offered, indicating specific ways in which you can apply samurai information to your own business and personal life. The samurai maxim "To know and to do are one and the same thing" means, with respect to this book: "To demonstrate that you know the skills laid out in *Fighting to Win*, use them, apply them, try them out for yourself."

Precisely like the training which the samurai received, this book is holistic. It is concerned with your full development as a fighter, inside and out.

The title of Part One, *Humming Arrows*, alludes to the samurai practice of indicating that the fight was on by firing two humming arrows high into the air. The three chapters in Part One focus on the important principles and techniques of seeing your opponent for what he is and moving forward to engage him.

Part Two is entitled *Shinjutsu*, meaning "the skills of the mind and heart." Samurai general Hyogo Narutomi said, "Unless you have mastered your mind and body you cannot beat your enemies on the battlefield," and that is the theme of these four chapters dealing with inner samurai skills. Once you achieve *ki ken tai no ichi*, "the complete unity of your mind, heart and body with your sword," nothing can defeat you.

Gi, "technique," is the title of Part Three. These three chapters are designed to increase your skills in achieving what you want in conflict situations in which you are at cross-purposes with someone else. Effective uses of power, applications of strategy and tactics, and how and when to strike are the outer samurai skills treated in Part Three.

Fighting to Win is designed to help you answer the following questions with a solid, unequivocal *yes:*

• Do you recognize the opponents that are barring your way to greater success in business and personal life? (Chapter 1)

• Are you always able to advance on your objectives without being stopped by self-doubt and the fear of taking a chance? (Chapter 2)

• Can you take the tough, hard realities of life's crises and gut punches in stride and still move forward with total commitment? (Chapter 3)

• Can you, like the samurai, "beat ten men with your spirit alone?" (Chapter 4)

• Have you developed the ability to devote 100 percent of your concentration to every task facing you, from solving a problem to selling a product? (Chapter 5)

• Have you learned how to overcome your greatest opponent—you—and to live a "worry less, achieve more" life style? (Chapter 6)

• Do you possess the ability to defeat fear, depression, anxiety, nervousness and other emotional blocks? (Chapter 7)

• Do you realize that you possess tremendous power and do you know how to use it to get what you want? (Chapter 8)

• Do you know what strategy and timing are in business and everyday life, and what you're looking for when you use them? (Chapter 9)

• Are you skilled at *katsujin no ken*, the samurai striking art of taking advantage of your opponent's moves? (Chapter 10)

These are all warrior's questions. If right now you can answer each of them affirmatively, you're living life to the hilt. But if in all honesty you cannot, you've got some fighting to do.

PART ONE

HUMMING ARROWS
The Battle Commences

1

Stepping onto
the Battlefield

"Test your armor, but only test the front."
*Hagakure**

Your Opponents

When was the last time you were in a fight?

Whatever you answered, you were probably wrong. It wasn't the time in the third grade when you bloodied the nose of that wise guy, and it wasn't even last week. It was this morning or a few minutes ago. You might even be in a fight right now, for all you know.

We are brought up to believe that fighting is the exception, a once-in-a-while thing, when all along it's the rule. From the first day of the year to the last, from morning to night, you're in one battle after another.

There are two types of adversaries you run up against constantly in business and personal life: outer opponents and inner opponents.

Your outer opponents are any forces, hindrances, blocks or obstacles in the world outside of you that you have to overcome or eliminate if you're to succeed in reaching your goals.

Anything "out there" standing between you and your peace, prosperity, and well-being is an outer opponent. People (when they block your

---

* *Hagakure* is a written record of the thoughts of samurai Tsunetomo Yamamoto (1659–1719) on the Way of the samurai.

way) and problems, tough situations, setbacks, crises and difficult tasks—all these are types of outer opponents. More specific examples are: a resistant sales prospect, a police officer about to give you a traffic ticket, a boss who's hard to get along with, skilled negotiators haggling with you over a contract, an associate who's after your job. A powerful business competitor is an outer opponent, as is a new product that's forcing yours off the market, or being broke, or getting fired and having to find a new job.

Every business enterprise has outer opponents, from a skilled competitor to a diminishing demand for a given product, and every person does too. All business people have outer opponents in their professional and in their personal lives. Nothing with any kind of life to it is free of opponents.

Just take a few minutes to start compiling your own list of things "out there" blocking your way to the best life you can imagine for yourself, and you might be surprised to see how long a list it can be.

Your Dragons

"The greatest warrior is the one who conquers himself."
Samurai maxim

Ask any small child what a dragon is and you'll get an earful of terror and horror. You and I both believed in fire-breathing dragons until we discovered that the only place they existed was in our minds, that they were merely products of our imagination. They only "lived" and had the power to frighten us because we granted them license to. They died when we revoked their license.

All inner opponents are dragons. They are no longer of the fire-breathing variety. They are now a different species entirely. But the effect of scaring us and making us draw back in horror is precisely the same.

• Many people turn down job promotions because they fear they might fail at the higher job. Others turn them down because of an unconscious fear of succeeding. Fear of either success or failure is a dragon.

Fear is a very common and particularly hideous dragon. It's not by accident that defeating the dragon of fear is at dead center of the samurai way of life: "The end of our Way of the sword is to be fearless when confronting our inner enemies and our outer enemies," said Tesshu Yamaoka, the nineteenth-century sword master.

• Some people find themselves getting pushed around a lot of the time. Like comedian Rodney Dangerfield, they "don't get no respect." But there is nothing funny about this dragon if it's yours.

• Still others constantly worry about the future. They continually raise frightening "what-ifs." What if they lose their job? What if the economy gets worse? What if the work force goes out on strike? Point out to them that it's a beautiful day and the sun is shining, and these people reply, "Sure, for now. But what if it rains?"

• The basis of all business, including the business of living, is making a decision and taking decisive action. If you have difficulty either deciding what to do or taking action, or both, you're up against powerful dragons.

Inner dragons are obstacles in you that prevent you from doing your best and winning your battles. Shyness, timidity, low self-confidence, self-doubt, destructive work and personal habits, problems in handling pressure, down-in-the-mouth negativism, laziness, an explosive temper, nervousness, worry, constant boredom, low energy, stage fright, procrastination, difficulty in concentrating on what you need to do, not knowing how to use your power effectively or how to strike your opponents, losing control, and living and working without strong commitments—this is just a partial list of inner opponents.

Start your own list by heading a blank piece of paper "Inner Dragons." Then jot down anything you can think of *in you* that's keeping you from experiencing greater success in any part of your life.

If you find your list growing a heck of a lot longer than you expected, don't get depressed about it. Depression is another inner opponent. If you fall into it, suddenly you have two adversaries to deal with—the one out there that appears to be causing it *and* the depression itself. Instead, just remember:

Any inner dragon that has control over you does so because you have licensed it to be in control.

> *Revoke its license and it loses its power over you—like that, just
> as the fire-breathing variety lost its power.*

Revoking the license of inner opponents that are plaguing you is what
the samurai called "striking through the dragon's mask." You'll do a lot
of striking through the dragon's mask in this book.

Always Assume the Frontal Position

"Take arrows in your forehead,
but never in your back."
Samurai maxim

The first step in samurai fighting in your business and personal life,
against both inner and outer opponents, is acknowledging if and when
you've got a fight on your hands. Sounds simple, right? Well, it isn't—
not necessarily.

Your own experience will tell you that people (and entire companies,
communities and countries, too) respond to adversaries, problems and
tough situations in very different ways. Think of people you know and
how they operate. More important, think of your own first response to
your opponents.

Some people completely deny there is an opponent. If there is a problem out there or a shortcoming in themselves they don't want to know
about it. When they hear a noise in the house at night they pull the
blanket up over their head. Others realize what's happening, but choose
to overlook it: "Oh hell, let it be."

The head-under-the-blanket reaction is *hakarai* in Japanese, or "sup-
pression"; the let-it-be response is *akirame*, "resignation."

The samurai approach is entirely different. It's not suppressing the
fact that you've got an opponent on your hands, and it's not resigning
yourself to that fact.

The samurai always takes the frontal *kamae*, or "battle stance,"
against his opponent. He faces him and holds the stance with calm poise
and patience until the time is right to strike. There is only one right way
for the samurai to die in battle, and that is with his head closer to the

enemy than his feet. The samurai is taught: "Test your armor, but only test the front."

Even when your enemies are coming at you from all directions—when you find yourself in a "one against many" fight—take the frontal *kamae*. Drive them all together, says the great samurai Musashi Miyamoto, as if you're stringing a line of fish. When you've got them hanging together, cut them down one by one.

Assuming the frontal position in all areas of your life is the samurai spirit and style of living. If there are opponents, inner or outer, confront them, no matter how ugly, frightening or formidable they are. Face up to what's out there, and face up to yourself, with all your fears, worries and frustrations. The moment to strike and to rid yourself of this thing in front of you will come, but not until you acknowledge it. Stand fast and look it squarely in the eye, your head erect, eyes forward. Don't avoid it or pretend it isn't there. There is no question that you possess the power and ability to overcome all opponents, as this book will show you. But you won't have the opportunity to use them unless you assume the frontal *kamae*.

Refusing to face a problem or a disturbing fact is an all too common self-destructive habit in business or personal life. Recently an interesting laboratory experiment was conducted on responses to stress situations. All the subjects were told that they were about to receive a painful electric shock. Some of them—let's call them suppressors, or *hakarai* subjects—tried to deny the shock by thinking or fantasizing about something else. Others—the frontal *kamae* respondents—chose to confront the shock. They wanted to get it over with, and felt they could do something about it, if only by getting themselves ready. Instead of choosing to remove their attention from the impending shock as the suppressors did, the "frontal kamaes" chose to concentrate specifically on what was going on in the laboratory or on preparing their bodies for the electrical charge. The *hakarai*, blanket-over-the-head subjects not only felt helpless, but their heart rate measurements showed that they actually experienced much more stress than those with frontal *kamae* reactions.

The samurai is always a pragmatist. He faces opponents because it's simply not worthwhile to refuse to. Life is like that laboratory experiment. It is full of shocks that you have the power to confront if you want to; and if you confront them, you'll feel less pain in the long run.

Kan-ken

No fighting skill is more important than seeing. In samurai swords-manship, physical power is considered the fourth most important ele-ment of skill, courage the third, and foot movements the second. The most important? *Ichi-gan*, "First, eyes." See your opponent and you've got a chance. Since you know you see for sixteen or eighteen hours every day, you might be thinking, "Seeing, huh. Well, I can skip this part. If there's one thing I've got down pat it's seeing." Maybe you're right, but then again . . .

The samurai "two eyesights" is *kan-ken*. *Ken* is looking; *kan* is "seeing into." Everybody looks; the fighter sees into, even if what he sees isn't very pretty.

There are a great many individuals and entire companies, too, who don't like the frontal *kamae* because it forces them to see. John is the head of a government agency who heard me talking about the frontal *kamae*, got excited about it, and saw an immediate application to his own operation. He contracted my consulting company to survey the attitudes of his agency's prospective consumers toward its services. This is a fine frontal-position thing for any organization to do, and I was happy to conduct the survey. What the results showed was that John's potential consumers thought very poorly of the agency. Outraged, John screamed, "Those ungrateful bastards. How dare they? They're not pay-ing anything, are they?" Well, in the consumers' view they were getting exactly what they paid for—nothing.

It was only after some hard talking that I got John to see that you can't go halfway with the frontal *kamae*. If you can't stomach what you might see, don't look. But if you refuse to look, if you pull the blanket over your head, don't blame anyone but yourself if someone steps out of your closet and beats you to a pulp.

Part of my job as an organizational consultant is to uncover problems and bring them to the attention of management. Whenever I do this I encounter two types of responses. Some people, the *akirame* (resigna-tion) sort, right off the bat recite all the reasons they can think of why the problem exists and *has* to exist: poor staff, not enough money, bad markets, etc. Other staff—the frontal *kamae* minority—respond differ-ently. Their attitude is "We've got a problem here and it's holding us back. Now what can we do to solve it?" This is a good, productive, problem-solving beginning from which we can set out to whittle the problem down to size.

Then, invariably, some *akirame* in the organization will find reasons why absolutely none of the solutions will work. "Our people would never go along with that." "It just won't work." "The time isn't right," etc. Then others of the *akirame* persuasion chime in, citing reasons, many of them farfetched, why absolutely no solution will work and why nothing should be done. "We haven't got time to deal with it." "Remember Bill? He suggested the very same thing right before he got canned."

For the fighter there is literally more to seeing than meets the eye. If you're a skilled warrior, I already know the kind of seeing you do. It is *sono-mama* seeing.

Sono-mama seeing is perceiving the "suchness" of things, seeing things as they really are. It's holding no illusions about your opponents, your position, or the circumstances of the battle. Nothing mysterious here; *sono-mama* is simply not kidding yourself.

Its opposite is *gen*, "illusion." That's the worst kind of seeing for the fighter to do. Do it and you wind up fighting windmill opponents, not the real ones. If you're Avis, you're number two. That's the "suchness" of the market situation. To pretend you aren't is *gen*. Blame the economy for your miserable performance when it's really your lack of sweat-and-toil hard work, and you're seeing *gen*, not *sono-mama*.

I know a man who was fired from one job after another. Every pink slip he received further confirmed his belief that companies are only out to exploit their workers. He made his fight with them, never stopping to realize that the opponent was not "out there" at all, but in his own shortcomings. All the while he was doing a lot of *gen* seeing and just about no "suchness" seeing. As a result, he was constantly fighting the wrong opponent.

I've had the pleasure of helping thousands of people learn how to set goals for themselves. When I first started, a real eye-opener for me was realizing that often what prevents people from reaching their goals is not an obstacle "out there," but something inside them: it is simply their hard-as-granite belief that life is somehow tougher on them than it is on other people. The most exciting moment always comes when they realize that what's holding them back is that *gen* attitude. Once they strike through that dragon's mask they're on their way.

One of the most famous cases of business *gen* seeing was the development of the Ford Edsel. Ford had decided to develop a more attractive medium-priced car. It conducted extensive market research on what specifically consumers were looking for when they moved up from lower-priced lines to slightly more expensive models. Also, as a key element of the campaign to promote the car, the company held a national name-the-new-Ford contest.

Then Ford created the Edsel. The problem was that while the manufacturer's designers liked the car, the public didn't. So much for market research. Every name suggested by the public was rejected, and the car was named after one of the family, Edsel Ford. While many reasons were given for the colossal Edsel failure, the common thread was that the company had seen all too clearly the car it wanted to manufacture, but had totally disregarded the information the public had given about the kind of medium-priced car it wanted to buy. Goodbye *sono-mama*, hello *gen*. This *gen*, illusion, seeing cost Ford $350 million.

Running away from the truth is a habit many people learn as children and continue all their lives. They enter the business world and become runners there too. Some people are sprinters, and not fighters, as long as they live. Sometimes they have never had the good fortune to learn that no matter what size you are, or what disadvantages you're under, if you're skilled and fearless enough you can win most of the time, regardless of the size and stature of your opponent, the seriousness of your problem or the bleakness of your situation. This inner "I can win this thing" confidence is what all great warriors, successful businessmen and other achievers have in common. You can begin to break the running-away habit right now by making a conscious choice to take the frontal approach to your problems and responsibilities.

Always assume the frontal position. Say it to yourself. It's a wonderful motto to remember because it can work for you whether "you" are a company the size of General Motors or Standard Oil—or a person. And it can help you deal with opponents of any size and description, from the huge once-in-a-lifetime crisis to the small, minor problem. My friend Dorothy used it to help herself enjoy the game of volleyball.

Dorothy was a pretty fair player and really enjoyed the game, but stopped playing. She gave all kinds of phoney *gen* excuses for quitting. Like many people, she had an almost boundless capacity for self-deception. As she talked to me about why she didn't play any more though she loved the game, she repeatedly mentioned "calling for the ball," the

"I've got it" signal to other players meaning "Stay away, I'll handle the return." Eventually she realized that the real *sono-mama* reason she was denying herself the pleasure of playing was her fear of being seen as too dominating, too pushy. Once she was able to take the frontal position and look her inner "what-will-other-people-think-of-me" opponent in the eye, she was on the road to defeating it. Now she is back to playing and derives tremendous joy from it.

Use Zan-Totsu Tactics

"When crossing marshes, your only concern should be to get over them quickly, without delay."

Sonshi†

Samurai tactics never vary. They are always *zan-totsu*, "close and strike." Take the frontal *kamae*, be aware of who or what your opponent is, then go in, *zan-totsu*. Don't bother regretting that there is an opponent in front of you; instead, find a certain pleasure in the fact, even joy: "When you meet calamities and rough situations," says *Hagakure*, the eighteenth-century handbook for samurai, "it isn't enough simply to say you're not flustered. Whenever you meet difficult situations dash forward bravely and joyfully."

Wear Light Armor *(Katchu)*

The samurai chose never to wear defensive armor. He wore only a light flexible mat made of bamboo and hide woven together. It wasn't because he was stupid, but because wearing only light protection matched the *zan-totsu* spirit of *always carrying the attack to the enemy*. Defensive armor is heavy and hard to move in. Offensive armor affords you little protection, but gains you the advantage of speed and

† *Sonshi* is the Japanese translation of Sun Tzu, the name of a Chinese military theorist who was highly regarded by the samurai and a particular favorite of warriors of the Minamoto and Taira clans.

maneuverability. Samurai were always to strike like bolts of lightning. Whatever or whoever your opponent, you are not there to turn and run away or to slow yourself down. Most people who get what they want from life are more offensive- than defensive-minded. Like the samurai, when they test their armor they only test the front. They make certain they have some protection, but literally don't try to completely cover their rear ends.

Where your mind is focused is the key to winning or losing, succeeding or failing. Of course you don't really wear armor. "Armor" is a symbol of your attitude toward your battles. If you go into action wearing defensive armor your mind is on protecting yourself from injury. You're concerned with escaping safely. When you wear only offensive armor your mind is focused only on *zan-totsu*, moving in and striking. You're fighting for the victory, not to avoid defeat. Different armor— different attitudes toward battle.

Zan-totsu has a larger meaning, maybe the largest. It means always engage life, never withdraw from it. Never back away from it for any reason—because you're afraid, or you've been hurt, or you're bashful, or bitter, puzzled, tired, sullen, dejected, hurried, worried, forlorn, suspicious, resentful, disgusted, guilty, apprehensive, angry, humiliated, etc., etc., etc. When you move *zan-totsu*, you let nothing stand between yourself and where you want to get. You always dash forward, bravely and joyfully, without delay.

Guidelines for Stepping onto the Battlefield

"You can prevent your opponent from defeating you through defense, but you cannot defeat him without taking the offensive."
                                                                      Sonshi

Whether you're up against an inner or outer opponent, business or personal, always assume the frontal position. Look at it *sono-mama*, without kidding yourself. Wear light armor and go in *zan-totsu*.

• Whenever you sense opposition, confront it. If something is blocking your way to the life you want to live in business or outside it, assume the frontal position and peer at the obstacle.

• Don't try to kid yourself by saying, "I know I'm being blocked, but I don't know what's blocking me." You *always* know what's blocking you; you *always* know who your *real opponents* are. All it takes is admitting it to yourself forthrightly. Kid your friends, family and co-workers with *gen* excuses for your defeats if you feel compelled to, but for God's sake, and your own too, never kid yourself.

• Never ignore an opponent. The only one that's got you is the one you won't confront. If you drink, eat, quarrel, sleep, spend or lose too much, or if your business competition is outmaneuvering you, you'll have a hard time getting things under control unless you first assume the frontal *kamae* and face up.

• Detach yourself slightly. To swing his sword the samurai needed some room between himself and his adversary, and the same is true of you in handling your opponents. You'll have a better chance of defeating yours if you put them "out there" where they belong, so you can look them over. Here is a special technique that you can use to make some fighting room between yourself and your opponents.

The Detachment Technique

Whenever you confront an opponent of any kind, inner or outer, don't see it as *your* opponent, but only as *an* opponent. Look at it unemotionally and dispassionately.

If a problem arises, refuse to personalize it. It's not *your* problem, just *a* problem. Put it an arm's length away from you and size it up objectively.

Say, "There is a company going bankrupt unless something can be done to save it. What can be done?"—not, "Oh my God, my company is going down the tubes. I'm a failure."

Say, "There's a fear of confronting a boss. How can it be handled?" Don't say, "I'm such a coward. I don't have the guts to stand up for my rights."

"There's a weight problem that's got to be solved." Not, "I've got a weight problem."

Do you see the difference? It's not *your* opponent, but just *an* opponent.

You can choose how you will think about your problems and other opponents all the time. Your power of choice is your greatest power. You'll win far more of your battles as soon as you start dropping the "I," "me," and "mine."

Select your response to the opponent. *We-jei*, the Chinese term for "crisis," consists of two characters: one is "danger"; the other, "opportunity." I'm certain that every person and every company on earth could be assigned to one of two groups on the basis of the *we-jei* character they see most vividly. Some see an opponent and notice only the threatening aspect. The danger dominates them. Others see the very same opponent and are able to respond to the chance it offers for victory.

Divide the opposing force into its two aspects, separating danger from opportunity. Look at each as clearly and objectively as you can from the frontal *kamae*.

"On one hand, the market for our product has dried up. On the other hand, our knowledge, skills and equipment could be redirected fairly quickly to produce X, for which there is a market."

"Okay, the plant has been closed and I'm out of work. But, too, I felt really stifled in the company and the job wasn't that great anyway. This could be the motivation I needed to make a positive change."

• Now choose to concentrate only on the opportunity aspect of the battle. Rivet your attention solely on how much better things will be once you defeat the opponent.

At the stroke of midnight one New Year's eve I kissed my wife and said, "It was a great year and I'm pleased as hell with it." She was dumbfounded because on the surface it had been an absolutely horrible year. Even death had not spared our family.

What I was saying was that I had exercised my core human right, my right of choice, and I'd chosen to see all the many things I'd learned from my "year of crisis." "Adversity in life is essential to training," said *kendo* master Jirokichi Yamada. It's worth remembering.

• Strike. The fighter fights. It's as simple as that. Having seen the opportunities posed by the battle, go after them with a strong, resolute spirit. Dash forward *zan-totsu*, close and strike. Stop whining and *do* something. Act. Be aggressive, not apathetic or beaten. Go forward joyfully, as *Hagakure* says.

Taking physical action is a wonderful way to handle most of your opponents. If you're so depressed you feel like staying in bed all day, cross the depression marsh by getting up anyway. Get out of your pajamas and put on some clean clothes. You'll feel better already.

Having trouble writing that report? Start crossing that marsh by sitting down and scribbling whatever comes to mind. Soon enough you'll be halfway through the report.

Afraid of calling that important prospect? Pick up the telephone and dial and you're on your way across that marsh.

Do one small thing at a time, but do *something*.

• Be prepared for assaults from yourself. Even the most powerful fighters experience moments of serious doubt and hesitation. Taoism (pronounced with a hard *d*, "*d*owism") is an Oriental way of life which teaches that a thing is always followed by its opposite. Unhappiness is followed by happiness, war by peace, etc. It also means that feelings of success and optimism will always be followed by doubt and fear. So don't be surprised when after a period of hitting on all eight you suddenly wake up to find yourself afraid, timid and worried. Just recognize that your feelings are totally natural; then get up and take the offensive.

Points to Remember: Stepping onto the Battlefield

• Quiet as it's kept, fighting is something you do every day—with both outer and inner opponents.

• The great warrior learns to defeat his opponents "out there" that are blocking him; the greatest conquers himself. He does it by striking through the masks of the dragons inside him, the most common of which is fear.

• "Always assume the frontal position" is a motto worth reminding yourself of constantly. However bleak your chances appear in a business or personal situation, tell yourself to take the frontal position. Keep your head erect, your eyes forward.

• Hold no *gen* illusions; see *sono-mama*, the "suchness" of things as they really are, even if what you see isn't very pretty.

• Close in and strike *(zan-totsu)*. Inner opponent or outer, it makes absolutely no difference: you will achieve more of what you want *only* if you carry the attack to the enemy.

• Follow the guidelines for stepping onto the battlefield and you're on

rung one of the samurai ladder. In particular, always remember that
every battle is a two-sided coin, with "danger" on one side and "opportunity" on the other. Take the coin in hand, flip it, then *always* call
"opportunity."

2

Leaping into Action:
Mo chih ch'u

> "The fighter is to be always single-minded with one object in view: to fight, looking neither backward nor sidewise. To go straight forward in order to crush the enemy is all that is necessary for him."
>
> Daisetz Suzuki

Quick Action in Kyoto and Washington, D.C.

Samurai Musashi Miyamoto had already defeated two of the finest swordsmen of the Yoshioka family *ryu* (school of swordsmanship) in a field outside Kyoto when a duel with a third champion was arranged for the following morning.

Suspecting treachery, Musashi arrived at the designated site hours early and climbed a tree to wait in hiding. Soon the Yoshioka master arrived and took his place. However, as Musashi had suspected, the master had not come alone. With him were ninety swordsmen of the *ryu*. They formed a protective circle around the master.

Musashi immediately jumped down from the tree, drew his long and short swords and attacked the ninety-one Yoshioka. He cut his way through to the master and finished him with a single lightning-fast strike. In one swift motion Musashi turned, and as quickly as he had entered the circle, he fought his way *out* unharmed.

On January 13, 1982, millions of television viewers watched Martin "Lenny" Skutnik dive into the icy Potomac River to rescue Kelly Duncan, flight attendant of the Air Florida 737 that crashed shortly after takeoff from Washington's National Airport.

You might recall the scene: the rescue helicopter hovering over the frigid waters, a life preserver dangling from a rope and bobbing between the broken ice floes, the vain attempts of the exhausted woman to hold tight to the preserver that would carry her to safety. Suddenly Skutnik plunges into the river, swims to her and as she sinks below the surface pulls her up and brings her safely to shore.

Later that evening Skutnik was interviewed on national television. When asked how the rescue came about he said that he was on his way home, saw that the woman needed help and so threw off his overcoat, kicked off his boots and dove into the river. It didn't matter to him that hundreds of people were standing around doing nothing but watching. Skutnik saw what needed to be done and he did it. That was all there was to it, he said.

The news interviewer, unable to comprehend that in fact for Skutnik that *was* all there was to it, asked such questions as "Why did you do it?" "Would you do it again?" "Are you sorry you did it?" I recall commenting to my wife that the interviewer didn't understand the Way of the samurai. For the person of action like Skutnik, second-guessing is totally irrelevant. There is something to be done and you do it—right away and without hesitation.

Mo Chih Ch'u Action

"If you walk, just walk. If you sit, just sit. But whatever you do, don't wobble."

Master Ummon

When there was a battle to be fought the samurai always did two things. It made no difference to him if he was up against one man or ten. First he drew his sword without delay, and then he *leaped* into battle.

When you leap against ten men, or into a problem, or toward your goals, you feel an exhilaration and a commitment that you don't experience if you merely walk into battle. The more you fear your opponent, the greater should be your leap in that direction.

Like the samurai's world, yours is the world of action. It is right there in front of you, perfectly ripe for you to win. Business is just another word for action—presenting a report, conferring with a co-worker, attending a meeting, or making a sales presentation. Or it may be internal, mental action—sifting through information or solving a problem.

The action ability of the samurai is captured best in the Chinese term *mo chih ch'u.* It has a very simple meaning, but an extremely important one: It means "going ahead without hesitation." It's not looking back once you have decided on your course of action. Do your deliberating, mulling over, planning and preparing for the action beforehand; and if you feel you must sprinkle in some fretting and worrying, do that beforehand, too. But once you can say to yourself "This is what I want to do," then be on your way immediately, *mo chih ch'u.*

Keep your eyes open and you'll see *mo chih ch'u* action all around you. The master of *kyudo* (the Way of the archer) doesn't consciously say to himself, "Okay, hand, release the arrow now." Instead, the arrow seems to release itself. One of the secret texts of *kyudo* says, "The release of the arrow should be done without thought, like a drop of dew falling from a leaf or a fruit falling when it's ripe."

O. J. Simpson was a wonderful *mo chih ch'u* athlete. The all-star running back didn't stop to think things over before deciding when and which way to cut. Instead, he was conditioned to spot open spaces and run through them without hesitation. "I just try to clear myself and relax my body," he said. "I can't be thinking about one element of it."

Anyone with little children has to be prepared for *mo chih ch'u* action. Watch a mother snatch up a glass of milk just as her baby's arm is about to hit it.

A friend and I were sitting on the side of a kiddie swimming pool in which my two-year-old daughter was wading. Suddenly she slipped and went under. I was in the pool and pulling her up before my friend, who had no children, had even moved a muscle. Being a father had conditioned me to be alert to possible dangers to my child and to act with lightning speed and without hesitation when she was in trouble. That's precisely the type of immediate, no-hesitation reaction that the samurai was trained to make a practice of at all times.

Mo chih ch'u is what the real pro in any field does. Think of the real pros in your company, or think of yourself if you're one. Pros say, "I did it because it just seemed right." They have simply developed an instinct, a knack for the right action and do it without stopping to ask, "Well now, how the hell should I do this?" Once they've decided what's to be done they do it *mo chih ch'u.* Their acts are as spontaneous as the release of the arrow by the archer.

Asking your boss for a raise, trying to solve a problem, looking for another job, or making a sales presentation to an important prospect who's been known to chew up salespeople and spit them out—actions range from the very simple to the extremely complex, but the principles guiding effective action are always the same, and leaping forward *mo chih ch'u* is one of them.

Four Main Blocks to Effective Fighting Action

"Man is created for movement."
Shissai

There are countless blocks to direct *mo chih ch'u* action in everyday and business life. The following four are the most common and serious ones. Saying they are serious is not the same as saying you can't over-come them if you want to. No block is a fate. It's only an indication that you have some work ahead of you if you wish to become a more highly skilled fighter.

Block 1: Being afraid to take risks.

The one constant factor in warfare is uncertainty. Three quarters of the things on which action is based are obscured by it. It's the same in your personal and business life, too. If you're not leaping right into action because you're afraid of taking chances you've got a block on your hands.

Block 2: Thinking too much.

The Chinese character for "cowardice" is composed of two symbols, "meaning" and "mind." The coward is one who finds too much meaning in things—he or she thinks too much. Many individuals and whole businesses do the same thing. If you believe you're thinking too much and that it's driving you away from instead of *to* action, this could be a block you'll want to overcome.

Block 3: Doubting yourself.

The easiest quality for a fighter to spot in an opponent is self-doubt. Certainly the experienced businessman can spot it. If your inner voice is constantly muttering, "Who am I, little old me, to attempt *that?*" you're up against the self-doubt block.

Block 4: Hesitating.

Respond to your opponent by waiting and you become a hesitater. It's easy for even an unskilled fighter to keep the hesitater in check, even if the latter possesses superior technical skill. If you often find yourself waiting (for your lover to call you up, for those orders to come pouring in, for that "just right" feeling before you act or for the "right" moment to start your life's big enterprise) instead of leaping into action, you might be on the way to becoming a hesitater.

Guidelines to Effective Mo Chih Ch'u Action

"Go to the battlefield firmly confident of victory and you will come home with no wounds whatsoever."

Samurai general Kenshin Uesugi
(1530–78)

If you've seen yourself in the description of any of the four main blocks to fighting action, you will be interested in the following guidelines. They are designed to help you develop direct *mo chih ch'u*, going-ahead-without-hesitation action in any area of your life.

1. *Risk Injury—Risk Defeat*

When I first met Bill, he was second in command of an organization with a work force of approximately three thousand people. His boss told me that Bill actually ran things. I felt it would certainly help my consulting with the organization if I learned what decisions Bill was contemplating. But when I asked him he snapped, "Decisions! I'm not making *any* decisions. I made that mistake last year." Here was a man three thousand employees looked to for direction and job security, and he didn't intend to make any decisions!

One of the more powerful blocks to committed action in personal life and business is the desire for certainty, the sure thing. I had run across another Bill years before. His name was Herman. I had one season of high school track under my belt when Herman tried out for the team and made it as a quarter-miler. He was a decent runner who worked very hard. The day of his first meet came and since the quarter mile was coming up, the coach looked around for Herman, but he was nowhere in sight. Eventually, though, the coach found him hiding in a washroom, his legs shaking, his face pale with fright. I'll never forget coach putting his arm around Herman's shoulder and walking him to the track, then saying only one short sentence, very softly, very kindly: "Herman, it's time to get your feet wet."

Let's not be too hard on Bill and Herman. They're just extremes of what is in fact the most popular approach to living and doing business: trying to reduce risks as much as possible. Don't run and you can't lose the race; don't make decisions and you can't make bad ones.

It could be that right now you too are hanging back from making a decision or taking decisive action in your own business or personal life.

You might be shying away from potentially rewarding, exciting and incredibly gratifying experiences because you want to avoid the injury or pain that might occur if things don't work out. You want to keep your feet bone-dry.

If hurt in a personal relationship, you may believe that the best way to avoid being hurt again is not to become seriously involved in the future.

Perhaps you would like to start your own business, but avoid doing it because you fear failure.

Or, you don't call a sales prospect because you can't stand the possibility of hearing another "No!"

In making corporate decisions, too, we try to factor out risk. We use our brains, mathematical decision models, decision trees, computers and gut experience. We try like the dickens to avoid taking any chances at all. We want guarantees that we—ourselves or our companies—will not be injured or defeated. Yet, this is a very wrong way of looking at business and living.

The samurai motto "Expect nothing; be prepared for anything" means you can never know with certainty that conditions are as you think they are or that events will work out the way you expect them to.

• You might be healthy now, and I hope you continue to be, but can you count on being healthy in the future?

• Maybe you have an excellent job now—responsible, high-paying, highly respected. But who is to say at this very moment someone "upstairs" isn't estimating the dollars that could be saved by eliminating your position?

• Your company reached record profits last year and its future looks rosy. Sure, the buggy industry was big too before the automobile was invented.

Searching for guarantees in life and business is looking at them from the wrong end of the telescope, looking at them ass-backwards. The purpose of business and everyday life is *not* to avoid risk but to maximize opportunity. And where do the richest opportunities lie? *Exactly where the dangers are greatest.* The best chances for total victory are always to be found where your chances of losing are also great. Knowing this warrior's principle, Sonshi advised generals to *look* for danger and put their troops dead-center in the middle of it: "Place your army in peril and it will survive; plunge it into dire straits and it will come out safely. It is precisely when your force has fallen into harm's way that it is capable of striking the victorious blow."

The samurai swordsmen who roamed Japan seeking out other masters to challenge saw exactly the same thing—victory is found close to your opponent's sword. They were not stupid or reckless, they simply realized that the greatest rewards lie one inch from the foe's blade. The truly successful businessman realizes precisely the same thing.

Early in his career, insurance tycoon W. Clement Stone sold exclusively to small accounts—a few dollars here, a few there. The turning point came when he faced the fact that what kept him from real success

was his fear of contacting big companies. As soon as he approached the
large accounts in spite of his fear, the big money started rolling in.

The samurai, Sonshi and Stone each came to the same conclusion: it is
only by edging yourself in close to defeat that you approach great success. Whenever *you* encounter your "deadly peril" situations, tell yourself, "I've got to edge in. I've got to play it closer to the sword blade."

2. *Think Less, Act More*

You're thinking too much when you spend an inordinate amount of
time anticipating what could go wrong. The awful "what-ifs" (What if I
blow it? What if I lose? What if something awful happens?) will drive
you into inaction—and maybe crazy to boot—if you let them. Constantly thinking that what you're doing is not the right thing to do, that
you should be doing something else; or that *it* is right but you're doing it
all wrong and should be able to do it better—are serious signs of thinking
too much.

Try to make it a point to remember the term *tomaranu kokoro.* No
small thing in samurai fighting, it has been called "the secret essence" of
the samurai Way. More important, it's relevant to you in *your* Way,
whatever that might be. It means "a mind that knows no stopping."

If you have ever seen a master swordsman in action, you've witnessed
tomaranu kokoro. Without once stopping he attacks, feints, cuts, slashes,
turns, leaps, spins and thrusts in a whirlwind of action. The reason he is
able to move so smoothly, effortlessly and quickly is that he is doing the
same thing in his head. His body moves without stopping because his
mind is *tomaranu kokoro.* His mind doesn't stop to worry, to ask "what
if" or, as in the coward's case, to attach too much meaning to things. It
doesn't stop for anything. It keeps moving and facilitates the movement
of his body.

Toraware means "caught," and *tomaru* means "stopping" or "abid-
ing." You might want to remember them too, because they help explain
why an awful lot of people and whole businesses are not as successful as
they have the potential and the right to be.

It's when your thoughts get caught *(toraware)* or stopped *(tomaru)* that
you have trouble executing an action. It's when your mind doesn't flow

from one thought to another but gets hooked or snagged that you are prevented from fully functioning in business or life.

Recall the last time you were upset or troubled. It was because your thoughts were caught or stopped; they didn't flow. They kept returning again and again to the bastard who screwed you up, for example, or that tough task ahead of you at the office, or the fear that you might not meet a deadline.

The art of swordsmanship lies in not having one's mind "stopped" with any object, according to shogun advisor Takuan (1573–1645). It's also the art of business; and the art of living, too. When your mind stops when you're in battle, Takuan adds, you're sure to be beaten. That goes for business and living as well.

Whenever you find your thoughts getting caught or stopped, tell yourself to remember *toraware*, "caught," and *tomaru*, "stopping." More important, tell yourself to get back to *tomaranu kokoro*, the mind that knows no stopping, and return to action.

3. Reject Self-Doubt

Self-doubt is a thinking-too-much, cowardice-creating problem. It begins the moment that nagging little inner voice starts whispering in your ear: "I'm not prepared"; "He's got me by the short hairs"; "I wish to hell I was somewhere else"; or the thousand other scary statements you make to yourself. Self-doubt is a scavenger, a jackal feeding on your sense of limitations; "He's more powerful than I am," "He's smarter than me," "He's a better businessman," "A better fighter," and on and on.

You're thinking too much and getting caught, *toraware* fashion, when you hang back from action because of credentialism—your own rigid, self-doubting belief that you can't accomplish something because you lack the formal credentials or qualifications. In this country, in and out of business, we are simply credential-crazy. There are credentials of:

- Age—"You're too old for the job," or "You're too young."
- Sex—"A woman can't do that kind of work."
- Race—"You want to go into competitive swimming? You know there are no great black swimmers."

• Diplomas and degrees—"Only a Ph.D. can handle this job. Where's your sheepskin?"

• Experience—"Who the hell are you to tell me? This isn't your field."

• Size—"All our men are tall sales types."

A credential is supposed to serve as a certification of knowledge and ability. If you've got the credential, you know and can do X; if you lack the credential, you don't know and can't do it. You and I both know this is sheer nonsense.

It isn't widely known, but new discoveries in many fields are often made by credential-lacking newcomers or outsiders. Edwin Land quit college after just one year. He devoted himself to inventing and eventually took out over two hundred patents, including Polaroid and the Polaroid camera.

A young clerk in a Swiss patent office, working alone in his spare time, wrote the "Special Theory of Relativity." He was not a scientist. He worked in no laboratory. Yet his article would change the entire field of science and the history of the world. His name? Albert Einstein.

Thomas Edison was the greatest inventor of all time. He had 1,093 patents to his credit and a large business empire. But having had virtually no formal education, he lacked the credential of even a grammar school diploma.

Samuel F. B. Morse was one of the most famous American painters of the first half of the nineteenth century. He was also disturbed about how slow the U.S. mail service was. Without any previous credentials in the field, he invented the telegraph and the Morse code.

Michael J. Owens, of Owens-Illinois fame, left school at ten, never learned to read blueprints, never understood the decimal system, never mastered the idea of the scientific method and had no knowledge of chemistry or physics. Yet he invented the first automatic bottlemaking machine, without which the bottling of anything on a mass-production basis would be impossible.

King C. Gillette was a traveling salesman who knew little about razors and practically nothing about steel. One morning while shaving with a dull straight razor he paused to think that there ought to be something better, something the public would buy. He went to a hardware store, bought pieces of brass, steel ribbon used for clock springs, files and a vise, and with them made the first safety razor for disposable blades. A product, a personal fortune, a company, and a new industry were started.

Land, Einstein, Edison, Morse, Owens and Gillette—they were all *yaburu*. A *yaburu* is a fighter who really shouldn't win because he lacks technique, but who destroys the enemy anyway. Look at a *yaburu* and you say, "No way." Take another look and he's won. Why? Because for what he lacks in technical skill he more than compensates in guts and courage. Every *yaburu* knows but one thing—to rush forward.

It's sad enough that others block your way because you lack credentials. It's sadder still when you internalize these blocks and limit yourself. If others prejudge you that's their problem. But don't prejudge yourself.

The key to all victories is to be found in one place, and only one place —your own mind. What you choose to think determines your success or failure in all your battles. If your opponents have control of your thoughts they've got you, whether they're outer opponents or inner enemies. "In combat, one must never be controlled by the enemy." That advice comes from *sodo*, the Way of the spear. So always be leery of thinking too much about "Who am I to attempt this?"

4. *Don't Hesitate, Just Move*

Having once decided on your course of action—in life generally and at each moment—all that is necessary is to execute the action . . . *without hesitation* and with *makoto*.

Makoto is the samurai precept of precepts and a concept of action that the Japanese of today value above all others. It is usually translated into English as "sincerity," but it does not mean sincerity in the sense of "I'm sincerely pleased with the meeting we had."

Makoto means putting absolutely everything you have, everything you *are* into an act—all of your heart, spirit, mind, and all of your physical strength *(chikara)*. To hold anything back in reserve or to hesitate in any way whatsoever is to act . . . insincerely.

Any samurai watching Lenny Skutnik dive without hesitating into the icy waters of the Potomac to save a drowning woman would have muttered one word in admiration: *"Makoto."*

In samurai swordsmanship there is a bold move that requires the fighter to leap forward with two long steps under the opponent's sword. It is not a difficult techinque, and if executed properly it can bring quick victory. If you hesitate at all your opponent will beat you, but if you move forward with no hesitation whatsoever, you should win handily.

The difference between success and failure with this move, as with actions in personal life and business generally, is not your technical skill. Many may possess the skill to make the strike, but only a few *do not hesitate* to use it.

The businessman who hesitates is the one who holds part of himself back instead of committing his whole self to an action. You have seen him. If you're doing battle with him the odds are on your side two to one, because he is only half there. But if it is you who's the hesitater the odds are with your opponent—if he's not one—even if he's not nearly as bright or as technically able.

Your blocks to action are slowing you down and barring you from victory. People have their own private blocks, and entire corporations have theirs too. The way to get rid of them is to break the habit of being afraid to take risks, thinking too much, doubting yourself and hesitating. Start by asking yourself *why* whenever you find yourself hanging back from action. Identify the block, then defeat it by leaping forward. Here are some methods that will help.

Three Practical Methods for Overcoming Blocks to Mo Chih Ch'u Action

"Approach the moment with the idea in mind that you're in the fight to the finish."

Mataemon Iso, *jujutsu* master

1. The Time-Limit Technique.

A useful method for handling any block is to set a specific and inviolable time limit for blocking. Worry about the risks, think too much, doubt yourself and hesitate all you want—but only for a specified period of time. When the time is up go right into action.

2. Acting in Spite of: A Wonderful Way to Unblock Action

You can act your way right out of any block to *mo chih ch'u* action absolutely any time you want to—by acting as if you're not blocked.

Let's use an example of a powerful action blocker. Recently a medical group published a list of the Ten Most Frightening Things to Man— falling forty-two thousand feet without a parachute, watching your child get hit by a truck, and so forth—and the number one fear turned out to be what? Standing in front of an audience . . . stage fright.

Imagine yourself in an audience observing a stage-frightened person. Even if you didn't already know he was afraid, you could tell just by watching him. He walks to the podium slowly and tentatively, as if it were the last place in the world he wanted to be. His head is bowed, his eyes down. His facial muscles are tense and tight. Afraid to begin, he stands at the podium shuffling his note cards. He shifts his weight from foot to foot and looks downright scared.

The situation is totally different if the would-be speaker chooses to pretend that he is not afraid. The moment he begins to act like someone who is totally comfortable making public addresses, he begins to feel comfortable. All he has to do is assume a stance and manner that is exactly like the battle stance of the samurai. He should stride confidently and quickly to the podium, head high, eyes on the audience, shoulders low, a relaxed expression on his face. Having reached the speaker's stand he should begin speaking clearly and more loudly than normal.

We used the example of stage fright, but the underlying principle is exactly the same, whatever the action involved. *The way to overcome a block to action is to act in spite of it.*

In *Go Rin No Sho (A Book of Five Rings)*, Musashi points out how to stand, look and hold your arms in combat so as to create a true warrior's spirit. The point he is making is one any fighter has learned: your spirit conforms to your body. *You feel how you act.*

If you act weak you will feel weak, but act strong and you will feel strong. Act scared and you'll feel scared. Act confused and you'll feel confused. But act bravely, as if you're totally cocksure about what you're doing, and you'll feel that way and *be* it too.

3. Move Faster

Get in the habit of deciding what you want to do and doing it decisively, whether it's taking a drink of water or negotiating an agreement or absolutely anything else. Naoshige (1537–1619), leader of the powerful Nabeshima clan, told his army of twelve thousand samurai: "When things are done leisurely, seven out of ten turn out poorly. A warrior is one who does things fast." *Hagakure* adds: "The Way of the samurai is immediacy. It is dashing in." Simply by *moving* more quickly and decisively you will do much less hesitating, thinking too much, self-doubting and risk-fearing . . . and much more doing.

If you feel hesitant about a meeting, stride strongly into the conference room and take your seat. What you fear most, get to first. The first *bushi* to reach the enemy is always accorded the highest honors.

If you've been putting off telephoning someone because of some block to action, snatch up the receiver and make the call. If you're a salesman who has trouble making presentations to powerful people, set up an appointment with the most important prospect you can find and walk proudly into his/her office, thrust out your hand and introduce yourself. If you need to, go off by yourself and practice exploding into people's offices.

Points to Remember: Leaping into Action—Mo Chih Ch'u

"How should a samurai behave in battle?"
"Go straight forward, wielding your sword."
Fourteenth-century advice
to a reluctant warrior

Mo chih ch'u is "going ahead without hesitation." It's the Way of warriors, go-getters and pros.

Being afraid to take risks, thinking too much, doubting yourself and hesitating are four common blocks to action.

War is the province of uncertainty, and so are business and living. Warriors choose to get their feet wet—risking injury and defeat—over playing it safe. They edge in close to their opponent's sword.

The Chinese character for "cowardice" is made up of two symbols, "meaning" and "mind." You can avoid thinking yourself into cowardice. Try to maintain *tomaranu kokoro*, "a mind that knows no stopping." It's when your mind gets stopped *(tomaru)* that you have problems moving.

Doubting yourself and worrying about whether you have the credentials will drive you right out of action if you let it; so will hesitation.

Makoto is putting your entire self into an action—all of your heart, all of your mind and spirit and every ounce of physical strength. It's operating with complete zeal, and without holding anything back in reserve.

Three particularly useful methods for overcoming blocks to action are:

- the time-limit technique
- acting in spite of
- moving faster.

3

Bushido: Living and Working at the Gut Level

"Focus on your purpose" *(Mokuteki hon'i).*
Japanese motto

Imagine a prehistoric man waking up in his cave and feeling a gnawing hunger in the pit of his stomach. No doubt he growled something that meant "I've got to do something about this." He rose from his mat of animal pelts, took his club in hand and left the cave to kill a beast for dinner.

It was a tough life, but one this early man could understand. His mission was obvious—to bring home the prehistoric bacon. His motivations to succeed, if only to live for one more day, were extremely powerful. This was operating at the gut level. It was living and working for a clearly understandable purpose, and laying everything on the line to serve that purpose.

The samurai, too, lived at the gut level. His job was to fight and to be prepared to risk *everything* in the process. He was literally fighting for his life, and this gave something to his life that helped make him extraordinary—*intensity.*

Anyone—absolutely anyone—operating at the gut level lives with an intensity that is completely unknown to the person who doesn't have a larger purpose to serve. The work and life of gut-level individuals are tinged with the intensity of fighting for one's life . . . Because that is what they are doing.

Run for Your Life

"The warrior's intention should be simply to grasp his sword and to die."

Kiyomasa Kato (1562–1611)

The story goes that a wise master and one of his students went for a walk through the countryside. The student pointed to a fox chasing a rabbit and said, "Oh, the poor rabbit."

The master said, "The rabbit will elude the fox."

The student was surprised. Maybe the old man's mind wasn't so sharp anymore. He said, "No, you see, the fox is faster."

"The rabbit will get away," repeated the master.

"What makes you think so?" asked the student.

"Because the fox is running for his dinner, but the rabbit is running for his life."

The first step in gut-level working and living is understanding that we are all rabbits and we are all running for our lives.

Whether wearing samurai armor or a business suit, the warrior is conditioned to act decisively in the face of inevitable fate. In his "Primer" for samurai, Shigesuke Daidoji says, "The idea most vital and essential to the samurai is that of death, which he ought to have before his mind day and night, night and day, from the dawn of the first day of the year till the last minute of the last day of it . . . Think what a frail thing life is, especially that of a samurai. This being so, you will come to consider every day of your life your last and dedicate it to the fulfillment of your obligations. Never let the thought of a long life seize upon you, for then you are apt to indulge in all kinds of dissipation."*

* Daisetz T. Suzuki, *Zen and Japanese Culture* (Princeton, N.J.: Princeton University Press, 1959), p. 72.

Hagakure says, "Every morning make up your mind to die. Every evening freshen your mind with the thought of death."

"Freshening" your mind with the thought of death might sound like a grim way to spend your time; on the contrary, it is anything but. Those who are totally aware of how short their life is—and who can feel the importance of that fact in their bones—live a completely different kind of life than the ones who drift along, never bothering to let the thought sink in that in a relatively short time they'll be gone. In Japan the samurai is likened to the delicate cherry blossom which doesn't last long in the wind that blows it from the tree. One moment it is there and the next it's gone. The same is true of the samurai . . . and you and me.

Every fighter chooses to die hard. If you're one you're no fool. You know death is going to get you, but it's going to have a battle on its hands. While alive, you're going to live, and without wasting very much of your time on being depressed, worried, afraid or putting things off for a tomorrow that might not come.

When you live with the full knowledge that death is on your trail and gaining ground, you feel a quick surge of energy, a sudden spark of vitality. When you live in the samurai style—*as if you were already dead*—you operate even more vitally. You acquire extraordinary courage and decisiveness. You're not timid any more, not about any thing, any task, any opponent. You reach a state of *seishi o choetsu*, "beyond life and death," where even the knowledge of your death doesn't frighten you anymore. All that matters now is making use of the *power* you suddenly feel inside to accomplish what you wish to and need to.

Ask Yourself Some Questions

Whenever an inner or outer opponent blocks your way, I want you to ask yourself two questions. You'll find that asking them is the most liberating thing you can do:

1. "What's more important in the long run, this opponent or my death?"

2. "Do I really want to squander the little time I have left being defeated by this opponent and feeling this way? Or do I want to use my time to reach my goals and to feel *good?*"

When you ask hard questions like these, you begin living like a warrior on the fringes of death. You remind yourself that death is always stalking you, and your every act takes on an intensity that was simply never there before. You live two notches higher and move three steps faster than everyone else. Immediately you start living at the gut level. And, when you do, you find that:

• You have incredible control over the conduct and quality of your life.

• Getting anything depends far less on being at the right place at the right time than on your decisions, commitments and efforts.

• Getting the breaks is nice; making your own is better. Some people are content to wait for the breaks, however long they wait; others—fighters—elect to advance, facing the issue, regardless of the breaks, confident of their ability to turn to advantage whatever may happen.

• You devote yourself to your survival and happiness and not to goals other people have established for you.

• You cannot be victimized by anyone else or by any circumstances unless you let yourself be.

• Your energy and endurance increase in proportion to your willingness to choose your own path.

• You tend to finish what you start because you don't start something that doesn't matter to you.

• You're able to change, to adapt, to find a way.

• There's no obstacle that you cannot remove through your own steady perseverance.

• You achieve your goals more often and sooner.

A Grizzly-sounding Exercise That Isn't

The following is an exercise that I have asked thousands of people to do. Some find it morbid. But the overwhelming majority of people don't. Like samurai, they are reminded by it of the value of living with intensity while they still can. One middle manager told me that performing this single exercise had snapped him out of the lethargy of business and life as usual. He said it was "the turning point in my life."

The exercise is a short one. Read this . . .

"How do you feel?" the first man asked.

"Like one who has risen in the morning and doesn't know whether he will be dead in the evening."

"But this is the situation of all men."

"Yes, but how many of them *feel* it?"

. . . and *feel* it.

Take the Gut Punches

"A fine power is always heralded by great pain."
don Juan in *A Separate Reality*

At times it takes a severe emotional blow, a gut punch, to get us to live at the gut level of total commitment and decisive action. The death of a loved one, for example.

This book is dedicated to the memory of my sister. Sharon died of cancer at the age of thirty-seven. She was a small, delicate woman who stood five feet tall and never weighed more than ninety-five pounds. But she had the will of a warrior. I'm sure she endured more pain on just one of her "bad days" than I have in my entire life. Yet even as she was dying she always retained what was always her—her courage and dignity.

One day I had a meeting to attend. I knew it was going to be a long, brutal negotiation, and I wasn't looking forward to it at all. On top of it, it was a rainy, miserable day and I had a long, boring ride to take.

Then I thought of my sister. I realized how much she would have given just to be able to get out of the bed and walk, how thrilled she would have been to be able to go anywhere, to be in the traffic of life again. Suddenly, my gloomy feelings about the meeting were gone. Immediately I *wanted* to go out in the rain, I *wanted* to get to the meeting so badly that no force on earth could have held me back from it.

When word came that my sister had died I felt a tremendous surge of energy and commitment to my goals and my code of living. Many of the hesitations, resistances and fears that had held me back from what was really important to me were suddenly gone. Death has been called "the great equalizer." To me, my sister's death was a great clarifier. It clarified for me the difference between small-*l* living and capital-*L* gut-level Living.

There are other types of gut punches that, like the death of a loved one, can lead you to living and working at the gut level.

"I'll never be able to live without her," cried my friend Eli when his wife filed for divorce. "My life is ruined."

What he found, in fact, was that there was life after divorce—and a rich, full one at that. The divorce pulled the rug out from under him, and the shock of falling woke him up! Since the divorce, his job performance has improved, he's gotten raises and promotions, and he has expanded his circle of friends. He travels more, has gotten back to his hobbies and has come to know his two sons far better than he ever did before the divorce.

Any type of loss can supply the jolt that rouses you from sleep. The loss of a loved one, of a marriage, a job, a promotion, a big order, a business, a home, a sense of security.

All samurai were injured or wounded sooner or later in their careers—painfully and at times almost fatally. It was only after a warrior's first serious wound that you could tell what his permanent value would be.

Gut punches are the most severe wounds you sustain on your own personal and professional battlefield. How you take them determines what your permanent value to yourself will be.

Gut punches might be hell to endure, but they could be just what's needed to wake you up to the fact that you have a choice to make. You can let the punch defeat you or you can let it help you discover new possibilities and new opportunities. You can turn any pain in your gut into a turning point in your life if you *choose* to.

Bushido

"When you see ordinary situations with extraordinary insight it is like discovering a jewel in rubbish."

Chogyam Trungpa

Every day was a battle for the samurai. The object of the battle was laid out for him in his *bushido*, his code of action. *Bushido* told him exactly what he was living and fighting for, and what his gut-level purpose was.

How many people do you know who are aware of their real bottom-line purpose, who know what they stand for? Go up to your best friend and ask, "What's your purpose in life?" At first he will chuckle. But when he sees you're serious, he will probably ask, "What do you mean, purpose?"

Social scientists have noted a general, pervasive feeling of meaninglessness in American society. They point to the breakdown of the institutions of religion, marriage, the family and law and order, and see in essence a mass of people who are adrift, without the solid foundation that the samurai had: a gut-level purpose to serve.

In business the lack of gut-level purpose often results in "worker alienation" and the infamous blue-collar blues and white-collar blues. There are blues for any kind of collar you wear.

Two major factors in worker alienation are a feeling of powerlessness and a sense of meaninglessness. We can easily come to feel disconnected from our work when we believe it lacks purpose and we feel powerless to change either the work or ourselves for the better.

Industrial study after industrial study demonstrates what you have to go no further than your own mind and spirit to discover: working people want a purpose. They need commitment.

Ask a samurai what his gut-level purpose is and he can tell you without the slightest hesitation. And that is precisely why he can act without hesitation.

The foundation of *bushido* was duty, *giri.* "Duty" means "what's due," what we owe. It is doing what has to be done without regard to pleasure or pain, liking or disliking.

Tomonobu Kamiyama was a samurai in the service of Katsuyori Takeda. Kamiyama took it upon himself to warn Takeda that his forces would suffer defeat unless he adopted a different course of action. For this, Kamiyama was banished and his name slandered. Yet, upon learning that virtually all of Takeda's forces had been defeated by the great general Nobunaga, Kamiyama raced to his former master's side and died with him in April 1582.

Lord Soma's book of his family's genealogy was his prized possession. One day Soma's mansion caught fire. Watching his house go up in smoke he said, "There's nothing in there that can't be replaced except the genealogy. My only regret is that I wasn't able to pull it out before I left the house."

One of Soma's samurai said, "I'll get it for you." His fellow samurai laughed because the volunteer had never been particularly useful to the lord. Soma said, "No, it's too late. The house is engulfed in flames." But the samurai insisted, saying "I've never been of use to you before, and I vowed to myself that I would make up for it some day. Today is the day." He then ran to the house and leaped into the flames.

Soma and the others waited, but the samurai never came out. When the fire was finally extinguished they searched for the body. They found it in a small garden outside Soma's bedroom. As they turned the body over, blood flowed from its belly. Inside the stomach was the genealogy, which from that day on became known as "the Blood Genealogy." To keep it from the flames the samurai had cut himself open and placed the book inside.

Forty-seven Samurai and One Salesman

"You must push yourself beyond your limits, all the time . . . the only possible course that a warrior has is to act consistently and without reservations."

don Juan in *Tales of Power*

"If your sword is broken," said Hyobu Oki of the Saga clan, "strike with your hands. If your hands are cut off, press the enemy down with your shoulders. If your shoulders are cut away bite with your teeth." This may sound extreme—but it shouldn't, not if you're serious about reaching your goals and defeating your opponents.

In 1700, Naganori Asano, daimyo (lord) of Ako, was insulted by Lord Yoshinaka Kira, an influential daimyo of the court of the shogun at Edo (present-day Tokyo). Asano drew his sword and attempted to kill Kira, but succeeded only in wounding him slightly. Drawing a sword inside the palace of the shogun was an offense punishable by death. This Asano knew. He accepted his fate and was granted the honorable samurai death of suicide *(seppuku,* or *hara-kiri).*

Forty-seven loyal samurai of Asano vowed to avenge his death by killing Kira, knowing full well that to do so would mean their certain death. The Code of One Hundred Articles (1650) prohibited an act of revenge by samurai unless the authorities were notified in advance and official permission granted.

The forty-seven samurai were faced with a moral dilemma. They knew that permission would not be granted against Lord Kira. At the same time, their *bushido*, the code of the samurai, told them, "Thou shalt not live under the same heaven nor tread the same earth with the enemy of thy father or lord." Their decision, which took them no time to reach, was to serve the higher law of *bushido*—loyalty.

Realizing that Kira and his samurai were suspicious of them and expected them to strike immediately, the samurai agreed to make it appear that they had no intention of taking revenge *(kataki-uchi,* or "vendetta"). To throw Kira off, they purposely disbanded and lived the lives of dissolute *ronin,* masterless samurai. They left their families and lived like drunkards and dishonorable men "who knew not *giri"* (duty). All of Edo expected vendetta, but it did not happen. Instead, the forty-seven lived like "dog samurai."

Before disbanding, the men had agreed to meet one year later and take their revenge. On the night of December 14, 1702, one by one the forty-seven appeared at the meeting place and together made a final vow to the memory of their lord Asano. Under cover of a snowstorm, they attacked Kira's stronghold and cut down all his samurai. They offered Kira the honorable death of *seppuku.* When he refused, they cut off his head with the same blade Asano had used to end his life.

As they left Kira's property and marched through the streets of Edo to Asano's grave they were cheered by throngs: people rushed out to see these men who knew the meaning of *giri,* duty at all personal cost. They continued to the grave of their lord and placed the head of Kira and Asano's sword there, along with a letter which read:

"We have come to pay homage . . . We could not have dared to come unless we had completed the revenge which you began. Every day we waited seemed like three autumns to us. We have escorted Lord Kira to you and returned the sword you entrusted to us. This is the respectful statement of forty-seven men."

All the samurai were tried and sentenced to death. Together they committed *seppuku* while in prison.

This story of the forty-seven *ronin* is the most revered event in Japanese history. It is known by all Japanese as *Chushingura* and *Shi-ju-shichi gishi,* "the forty-seven faithful samurai."

Serving a purpose doesn't have to be as dramatic as the story of the Blood Genealogy or of the Forty-seven Ronin—thank God. It can take the form of the steady, unrelenting push of everyday work.

In the late thirties Heublein bought the American franchise rights to Smirnoff Vodka. In 1939, Heublein was selling a mere six thousand cases of Smirnoff a year. After World War II, a man by the name of Eli Shapiro was hired as the Smirnoff salesman in California, and it was Eli's determination and persistence, fueled by a refusal to knuckle under to defeat, that almost single-handedly accounted for the growth of Smirnoff.

Since he was not representing a major company or a known brand, Shapiro had tremendous difficulties getting in to see liquor store owners, wholesalers and restauranteurs. What he lacked in clout, he made up for in will power. At times he would wait hours to see a prospect, only to be told that the buyer didn't have time to see him. There would be Eli back the next day—and the next and the next. He knew he had a good product that would sell itself if only the prospect would try it. Because of his persistence that's exactly what happened most of the time. Eventually the prospect would give in, buying a few cases on a trial basis. Eli developed thousands of accounts this way through sheer samurai-like perseverance. By the late 1960's Smirnoff was established as a giant—the second largest liquor brand in the United States—with sales of over seven million cases a year.

Strike with *Isshin*

As soon as you know what your purpose, your own *bushido* is, and begin to operate with a complete commitment to it, your every act takes on tremendous power, a power strong enough, as the samurai says, "to bring down a wall of iron."

All samurai are conditioned to strike with *isshin,* "one mind." It is tackling every battle, every task, every responsibility single-mindedly—with only it in mind.

The opposite of *isshin* is *zanshin*, "remaining mind." It's holding back on your commitment to the fight and not giving it your all. For example, many otherwise very professional salesmen have difficulty asking for the order. They might be masters at making the presentation and laying out the benefits of purchasing the product, but when it comes time to ask for the signature on the dotted line they either don't ask or become very inept. Why? Fear of rejection? Or because they want to be seen as nice guys and they believe nice guys don't ask a person for money? Either way that's *zanshin*, "remaining mind."

Wanting to be the life of the party but letting shyness hold you back —that's *zanshin* too. Longing to start your own business but allowing your always-play-it-safe approach to life prevent you is *zanshin*.

It's known equally well in the East and the West that the people and the corporations who make the fullest use of their talents and accomplish the most are those who devote themselves single-mindedly to their goals. They're "isshins," not "zanshins." Power of action comes from always closing ground on your goal with a focused *isshin* intent. To demonstrate to yourself the power of focused intention, try these simple *aikido* exercises:

First, walk past someone and think "behind you." Think, "I wish I could stay at home," or, "I'd rather be doing something else." As you pass the other person, have that person raise an arm in front of you. If your thoughts are behind you, you'll be knocked back easily, even if the other person uses only a minimum of strength.

Now do the same thing again, but this time think *forward*. Think, "I must get where I'm going," or "Nothing under the sun can stop me." When the other person's arm is raised to block you, you'll walk right through it.

The point of these exercises is this: when your mind is clear of any reservations about where you want to get, you tend to get there.

When you have your own purpose for living, your own *bushido*, and you're totally and unhesitatingly committed to it, amazing things happen to you. All your mental and physical power and skill is brought together and concentrated on achieving what you want. It is all there with you and you're operating at the gut level. You suddenly become aware of who or what your opponents are and you want to be rid of them. If carrying out your *bushido* requires you to take risks, you suddenly *want* to take them. You realize that if you hold anything back *(zanshin)* you rob yourself of power.

Life is short. There is nothing to fear and no reason to hold anything back. Always, always, always *Mokuteki hon'i*, focus on your purpose.

Find Your Personal Gut-Level Bushido

"He who has a why to live for can bear almost any how."
Friedrich Nietzsche

When you're totally committed to your pursuits, whatever they might be, you're following "the *bushido* path." It's choosing the *bushido* path, time and again, that makes the fighter different from the person who's merely drifting along in life. What is the *bushido* path?

It's the career or life task, the Way that you feel you must follow, perhaps even the course you feel you were destined to follow. It's called *shinjin* in Japanese—the real you. It's the opposite of working just for a paycheck, or keeping the real you an arm's length from your job or everyday activities. You're on a *bushido* path when there isn't an inch of difference between what you do and who you are.

Comedian George Burns was once asked what acting was all about. Reportedly he replied, "The secret of acting is honesty . . . If you can fake that you've got it made." You can fake a lot of things, including honesty, but one thing you can't fake is gut-level commitment.

It's not necessary that my purpose for living, my personal *bushido*, be important to you: just as it isn't necessary that yours be what I would pick. What matters is that your gut-level purpose, your *bushido*, be yours.

• The first step is defining your personal *bushido*. Ask yourself what you want to live for day in, day out. What do you want to stand for? It may be, for example, becoming the best businessperson you can become, being a good provider for your family, bringing happiness to others, raising your kids well, expanding your business, inventing a new product, providing secure employment and safe working conditions for your employees or completing your education. There are any number of *bushido* paths. All that matters is that you clearly understand what yours is.

• Apply the Law of Give-up-to-Get. This law applies to corporations and individuals, to personal life and business life too. It simply means that to be fully committed to something—to strike with one mind—you have to sacrifice other things. To reach an important gut-level goal, you have to stop chasing other possible big goals—at least temporarily. It's a law that isshins (total commitment people) understand, but it's lost to zanshins.

To apply the Law of Give-up-to-Get, take a good hard look at what your real *bushido* goals are. Then decide what you will have to sacrifice to reach your real gut-level goal. Don't kid yourself. Hold no illusions. Sacrificing anything is hard. Most of us and most corporations want everything all at the same time. When you apply the Law of Give-up-to-Get you become a kind of pruning shears. You snip off what's holding you back.

• Remind yourself every day what you're living for, and devote the day to it. Before you begin your day's work, state your *bushido* to yourself. If yours is to make as much money as possible, say, "Today I will devote myself to bringing in as much money as I can." If it is to bring greater peace and tranquillity into your life, say, "I devote this day to finding harmony in all things and to a relaxed, balanced living."

• At a certain point during the day, stop the action and ask yourself if in fact you're living your *bushido*. When you devote your day to your *bushido* you make a contract with yourself. Are you living up to the contract or not? If you find that you're straying off course, start anew immediately and get back on track. Refocus on your purpose.

• At the end of the day ask yourself if you lived the day the way you hoped to. If you did you'll feel a justified satisfaction. If you didn't, commit yourself to living closer to your *bushido* from that point on. Commit yourself to it and begin again.

Points to Remember: Living and Working at the Gut Level

• Focus on your purpose always *(Mokuteki hon'i)*.
• Remember you're running for your life, so *freshen* your mind with the thought of death.

• The severe emotional blow—the gut punch—is a law of living. How you take your gut punches determines what your permanent value to yourself will be.

• Strike with *isshin,* "one mind," and you'll win most of your battles. And you will bring down your walls of iron.

• Find your own personal *bushido*—not mine, not your neighbor's or anyone else's. Yours. Follow it along the *bushido* path and you will live with a tremendous power of action. Don't take my word for it. See for yourself.

PART TWO

SHINJUTSU

The skills of
the mind and heart

4

Ki
The Spirit
of the Warrior

"Fill yourself with *ki*" *(Ki o mitasu).*
Mataemon Iso, jujutsu master

For centuries Eastern warriors have sought to cultivate an extraordinary form of personal power. It is called *"ki"* (pronounced "key") in Japan, *chi* ("chee") in China and *prana* in India. We really have no one word in English that adequately conveys the full meaning of *ki.* Approximations include energy, spirit, aura, vitality, breath, life force and inner strength. It's simply *ki.* Like the businessman or anyone else living at the gut level, the warrior doesn't really care very much what something is called, but only if it actually works and, if it does, how to make it work for him.

After learning how a person could generate *ki* through simple, practical exercises, one night I actually tried it. The next morning, before boarding a commuter train to take me to a lecture I was to give, I tried it again. I felt as though I were floating two inches off the ground the whole day. I experienced an energy and power I had never known before. The day went beautifully, almost blissfully. Everything was absolutely right. It wasn't only that my mind was sharp: the energy was simply phenomenal.

Some time after that I had a breakfast meeting with a business friend of mine. He told me that he had been "off" recently. He was going through a rough period. He had a hell of a lot of work to do, hard decisions to make, and was operating under a lot of pressure. But try as he would, he simply could not get himself together, and the work was piling up.

All I did that morning in a short fifteen minutes was describe my experience with *ki* and suggest how he could develop his own if he wanted. Writing on a napkin, I outlined the steps he could follow. They were the very same steps you'll find in this chapter. We paid the check, left, and that was that.

Two weeks later he telephoned to thank me.

"Thank me for what?" I asked.

"That *ki* business," he said. He went on to tell me that since we had talked that morning he had experienced the most fruitful two weeks in his entire life. After our breakfast he had gone to his office and immediately taken out the napkin and followed the steps. "I haven't been the same since." Decisions he couldn't make before, he was now able to make easily. He had felt heavy and listless before; now he felt strong and energetic. What had seemed like insurmountable problems before suddenly had become mere stepping stones to progress.

Those experiences with *ki*—my own and my friend's—taught me that even a minimum of information about this unusual form of power can lead to positive and sometimes extraordinary changes in a person's life. It's a learning that's been confirmed many times since.

What my friend and I had experienced for ourselves were two features of *naiki,* the samurai "doctrine of *ki*" and of all fighting: energy and mental control. We had learned that if you use your mind and body in a certain way you can create an unusual form of energy field.

Ki is universal—everyone has it. Right now *your ki* is:

1. energy
2. a frame of mind or attitude
3. a force that affects other people, and sometimes very powerfully.

1. *Ki Is Energy*

"The main thing in fighting and living is for your *ki* to be strong
and lively."

Shissai

Psychotherapist Wilhelm Reich used the word "streamings" to describe energy in the human body. He said that at times streamings flow, and other times they're dammed up. They flow when you're optimistic, when you're not tense or worried. When they flow you experience an inner glow. You have a completely new sense of courage and self-confidence. Reich's concept, "streamings," may seem strange to some people, but it certainly wouldn't to the samurai. He would call it *ki* and state that what Reich says it does, it does. And modern technology is helping to prove that the samurai and Reich were right.

According to a research project undertaken by M.I.T. in 1978, there actually is an electrical energy field around the human body, and it can be regulated in exactly the way the samurai regulated it—by breathing in a particular way.

Ki is very closely related to breathing, and that's why it's sometimes translated as "breath." The M.I.T. research demonstrated that the breathing exercises used by the samurai in fact thicken the energy field. Everyone has a *ki* energy field around him, but martial arts practitioners using *ki* breathing techniques actually have a different kind of field than the average person. Using modern photographic processes, the field can even be seen!

In one of the most amazing demonstrations of *ki*, Kirlian photography was used to film *karateka** Teruyuki Yamada breaking a one-inch board with a *ki*-powered blow. Now there's nothing amazing about a punch breaking a board. *But it is amazing that the punch never hit the board.* Playing the film in very slow motion revealed that the board actually snapped when Yamada's fist was still an inch away from it. What had shattered the wood was the pressurized force of the *ki* field between the board and the fist!

Ki is also curative. For centuries Chinese healers have used their knowledge of *chi* to manipulate its flow in sick patients. Physicians in

* The suffix "ka" means "practitioner of." "Karateka" thus means "practitioner of karate."

various Western countries are currently experimenting with electrical energy stimulation to heal a variety of body injuries, often with extraordinary results. Soviet sports scientists photograph streams of electrical energy in and around athletes' bodies, then use lasers to stimulate its flow to heal injuries and treat fatigue and emotional disturbances, such as depression and anxiety.

2. *Ki Is a Frame of Mind*

"First see to it that you, yourself, are all right, then think of defeating an opponent."

The Way of the spear

Ki is more than energy. It's an attitude, a frame of mind. Your frame of mind and your *ki* are basically one and the same thing.

The samurai was first and foremost a superb warrior. But he was something of a psychologist, too—a psychologist of fighting. He knew that three things always go together, like three peas in a pod: frame of mind *(shin)*, energy *(ki)*, and physical power *(ryoku)*. The magical (and practical) formula of *"shin* makes *ki* makes *ryoku"* was true for the samurai and it's just as true for you.

• Ever try to hit a golf ball (or make a speech, type a letter or cook dinner) when your mind was preoccupied with something else? Sure you have. And you probably performed awkwardly. The samurai found exactly the same thing: "If your mind is preoccupied, your *ki* tenses, and you become awkward." Preoccupied mind, tense *ki*, awkward golf shot—it happens all the time.

• Ever been afraid that your job was in jeopardy, or that you wouldn't have enough money to pay the bills? One thing you *didn't* feel was powerful. "The *ki* of the fearful person is meager." Fearful mind, meager *ki*.

• Have you gone to a party or a meeting or to see a sales prospect thinking, "I don't make a good first impression?" In all likelihood the impression you made was not a very good one. Most of the time what other people think of you is determined by what you expect them to think of you—by your *shin* and *ki*.

It makes not one bit of difference if the other person is a n̶ ̶̶
prospect or a stranger in a cocktail lounge or if it's five hundred people
sitting in an auditorium to hear you speak—if you just assume that they
are going to like you and you act as if that's true, you're going to be
proven correct almost every time. But it works in reverse too. Assume
that the other person is *not* going to like you—that he's nasty or a cold
fish, and act as if he is, and you'll be correct just about all the time. For
the samurai, "Form follows *ki,* and *ki* follows the mind."

You know very well that if your thoughts are irritated or confused—if
you're "off"—your commitment to action is not 100 percent and your
spirit and energy are weak. But when you know exactly what you want,
and what you have to do to reach it, you're able to devote yourself to
doing it with a powerful singleness of purpose. When you're like that,
your *shin, ki* and *ryoku* all working together, there is almost no way of
stopping you.

What separates winners from losers? What differentiates Olympic
athletes from other world-class competitors? According to a group of
scientists who have been studying America's top wrestlers, the difference
is not in physical ability. And it's not in training methods: they're pretty
standard. The difference is in the athletes' *frame of mind,* their *shin*—in
what they choose to think.

Men who were eliminated in the 1980 U.S. Olympic trials tended to
be more confused or depressed before the match—that's very bad *ki*—
while the winners were positive and relaxed. Those who made the
Olympic team were also more in control of their reactions than the
losers, who were more likely to become upset emotionally. Without even
seeing one wrestling match, the scientists were able to predict 92 percent
of the winners by using profiles of the athletes. A positive, optimistic
frame of mind *(shin)* increases energy *(ki)* and creates explosive power
(ryoku). On the other hand, a negative frame of mind reduces your
energy and cuts down on your power.

Feeling free and easy, being relaxed and calm, not being caught up in
problems or worries, thinking positively and optimistically, expecting to
do well, being committed to what you're doing, not being grumpy or
irritable, feeling fearless, buoyant and confident . . . all these are positive *shin,* positive *ki, ryoku* power-producers.

Experiencing depression, anger or hostility, losing heart, being afraid
of something lying ahead of you, worrying, expecting defeat, holding a

grudge, feeling timid or uneasy and being confused in action . . . these are examples of negative *shin*, negative *ki*, power-depleters.

Think of your own friends. Some are lively and flexible "up" people; others are constantly down. The former are positive-frame-of-mind, positive *ki*, explosive-power people. The others are negative-frame-of-mind, negative *ki* and low-power people.

I have two business friends, Jack and Bob, who are very similar with respect to intelligence, ability, knowledge and experience. They grew up together. They even look alike. However, in spite of their many similarities, they're very different. Jack is depressed easily, and sees work life (and personal life too) as something one has to suffer through. Bob, on the other hand, is amazingly buoyant, energetic and optimistic. Both men have suffered setbacks in business and outside it, but they react to them very differently. Jack dwells on his. He complains and becomes grumpy and irritable. Bob picks himself up, and in the samurai spirit of falling and rising again, he reenters the business or personal fray without hesitation.

Jack endures his job the way one endures a dread disease. He's been employed by the same company all of his working life and yet he hasn't been promoted very rapidly. He feels he's going nowhere and he's probably right. He has told me more than once that whatever he touches turns to shit.

Whatever Bob touches turns to gold. He moves quickly from one success to another. After a meteoric career with a large international firm he bought his own company. At the time it wasn't solvent, but in a few short years Bob had transformed it into one of the most successful businesses of its size in the country. He sold it at a hefty profit, and over a four-year period started three other businesses, each of which he runs, and each of which produces a sizeable profit.

The major difference between these two otherwise similar men is the difference in their frame of mind; or, as the samurai would put it, the difference is in their *shin*.

Because their *shin* is very different, so is their *ki* and *ryoku*. Bob's *ki* is positive and his power of action is all right there, 100 percent. Jack's *ki* is negative and his power is almost nonexistent. Their *shin* is a difference that makes *all* the difference. It's quite possible you know a Bob and a Jack. The world is full of Bobs and Jacks.

Infused with *ki*, the samurai was able to perform extraordinary physical feats by directing his *ki* into the physical power of *ryoku.* This fed amazing power into his sword strike, just as today it enables martial artists to break slabs of wood, brick and stone, and just as it will enable you to increase your power of action, *whatever* that action is—be it making a sales presentation, having a good time at a party or handling situations in day-to-day life.

3. *Ki Is a Force That Affects Other People*

Ki is energy and it's your frame of mind. It's also *a personal force that you communicate to other people.*

Everyone has *ki.* Some people have a hell of a lot of it. You can *feel* their power when you stand next to them or merely look at them. They're something special and you know it immediately.

An important principle of *ki* is that positive creates positive and negative creates negative. Positive *ki* optimism—warmheartedness, self-confidence and courage—generates an aura of positiveness around you that others respond to in positive ways. Negative *ki*—grumpiness, anger, hostility, meanness and weakness—creates a negative aura around you that you can actually feel, and that others can feel too. It creates negative responses from people you come in contact with.

A person with weak or negative *ki* seems to others to be unpleasant, irresolute, diffident, or a pushover. The businessman (or businesswoman) with weak or negative *ki* inspires confidence in no one, whether it's his own staff or customers. In fact, he turns people off. He annoys and irritates them. People aren't happy being with him, and if they can they avoid him. The salesman with negative *ki* might just as well not expect to be salesman of the month. But the person with positive *ki* has the ability to move and enliven others, to inspire them, to stir them to action.

• "Chemistry" is *ki.* We often speak of the "chemistry" between ourselves and others. To the samurai, it's caused by the transmission of *ki* between people. Most of us have had the experience of meeting and immediately liking a total stranger. There is just that spark—the feeling of affinity, the powerful sense of liking that person. On the other hand, we sometimes encounter people with whom the chemistry is bad, the *ki* is negative. We just don't like them.

There is chemistry in the business world too. Rosabeth Kanter studied the factors leading to managerial advancement and success in large corporations. What was the most important factor? Was it professional ability? No! The key factor was *personal chemistry*.

Positive chemistry is another word for charisma, which is also a vital element of business management. Even though the top leader has control over the organization's rewards and punishments, he will excite more support for his policies if he is able to generate charisma, or what we call positive *ki*.

• Effective *communicators* and *persuaders* have high *ki*. Whenever people communicate, *two channels of message transmission are open*. The first is the channel carrying the meaning of the words being spoken. The second channel carries *ki*. Westerners normally pay far more attention to the first channel and often show little regard for the second. Yet it is very possible that the second channel, the *ki* channel, is at least equal in importance to the first and perhaps *more* important.

During several years of training tens of thousands of people, it has become clear to me that the second channel has a far more powerful effect on people than the first. If the trainer has good, positive *ki*, and like the samurai swordsman is lively, buoyant, energetic and optimistic, the people being trained will be charged up, will have confidence in what is being communicated and will actually learn more.

The cutting edge of any business is its ability to bring in money through sales. And how does the salesman get the prospect to make the decision to buy except by transmitting the message that "my product will benefit you more than your money" along the verbal channel, *and* "I'm an honest, trustworthy person you want to buy from" along the second channel? Find an extraordinarily successful salesperson and you *may* find a person with good sales technique, but you *will* find a person with exceptional *ki*.

The transmission of second-channel power also occurs in the bedside manner of physicians. The corporate equivalent of the bedside manner is the machine-side or desk-side manner of supervisors and managers. One study after another is demonstrating that the *shin* of the boss, his or her positive expectations about the ability of the subordinate to do a good job, is more important than the subordinate's aptitude for the job in bringing out high performance. These positive *ki* bosses, with their positive expectations, communicate "You *can* do the job," and their workers or subordinates *do*, even if on paper they lack the ability.

It's the same with parents. A study recently revealed that IQ or aptitude tests and teacher evaluations were less closely associated with students' success in math than parents' expectations—parents' *shin.*

How to Increase Your *Ki* and *Ryoku* Power

"There's something that makes a great athlete great. And I'm not sure it's physical talent. I think it comes from within."

Mike Ditka, football coach

A major part of samurai training, an inner aspect, was not concerned with increasing the fighter's technical abilities at all, but with making a strong, lively *ki* more available to him. *"Ki o mitasu,"* the samurai is told: "Fill yourself with *ki.*"

How can you *ki o mitasu* so that you have more energy and action power, a more positive frame of mind, and the ability to make a stronger impact on other people?

There are just three main steps that the samurai followed, the same three, incidentally, that I outlined for my friend on a napkin that morning over breakfast. They are:

1. Transmit your *ki* by filling your mind with positive *ki, ryoku* power-producing thoughts.

2. Focus your mind on a particular place on your body called "the one point."

3. Practice deep abdominal, or diaphragmatic breathing.

1. Transmit Your *Ki*

Any number of events happen to us that seem to provoke anger, annoyance, frustration and worry. Think of the jerks you run into, or the mistreatment, disrespect and deceit you receive from other people from time to time. There often seems to be someone out there trying to screw up your happiness. And think of the disappointments and hard gut punches you're forced to take every once in a while. At times it might seem that you're not moving down the field at all, but that you're being thrown for one loss after another; that your life in and out of business is a series of fourth-down, long-yardage situations. Automatically you're filled with negative *ki* and losing *ryoku* power—unless you make a deliberate effort to transmit your *ki.*

Some people, bless them, seem to be born with the ability to think pleasant, courageous, power-producing thoughts just about all the time. I know people like that, and so do you, probably. For those of us who were not so fortunate as to be born with a predisposition to think upbeat, optimistic thoughts, doing so requires the effort of *conscious choice.* Our job is this: to choose to think optimistic, *ryoku* power-creating thoughts instead of unpleasant, strength-sapping ones. It means catching our mind looking for the negative side of things, stopping it, and then making it jump over to the positive, the optimistic, the powerfully charged.

It means creating new thinking habits by choosing—consciously and deliberately—the thoughts we will think.

• Gloria, an artist, used the "positive *shin*–positive *ki*–powerful *ryoku*" formula to put on a successful exhibition of her work. She positive-*ki*'d herself right into big sales of her paintings.

• Mike, normally a glum fellow, used it to approach scary job interviews more optimistically.

• Jim applied *shin-ki-ryoku* to overcoming his fear of public speaking.

• Diane used it whenever she met defeat at the hands of her diet.

Make positive *ki* choices time after time and you will actually feel energy and power filling every nook and cranny of your being. The following are specific strategies that will help.

Strategies for Transmitting Your Ki

"If your *ki* is settled, your actions will flow."

Shissai

• To begin, become more aware of your thought habits. In general, do you think *ki*-creating, *ryoku* power-producing thoughts or are you often in a negative *ki,* power-depleting frame of mind? Some people can tell you right off the bat: "I have to admit it, my mind is like a record playing a funeral dirge. I'm always looking at the negative side of things —complaining, bitching, getting mad, thinking of all the things that could go wrong; not what good things might happen. Am I happy people can't hear what I'm thinking!"

But many simply don't realize how much negative *ki* they're creating. To find out for yourself, a useful technique is to stop the action for five minutes once a day and write down your thoughts as they pop into your head. Do this for one straight week or whenever you think of doing it. After you've filled a few sheets of paper put a plus sign after each positive *ki* thought and a minus sign after each negative thought you've listed.

Apply the following rule of thumb in grading your thoughts: any thought that creates power, good chemistry with others, optimism or forward movement gets a plus; and any thought that diminishes your power, creates bad chemistry, is pessimistic or prevents you from moving forward toward your goals and responsibilities gets a minus.

After you have graded the thoughts on your list plus or minus, ask yourself, "Which predominates, positive or negative?"

• Reject negative *ki* thoughts and replace them with positive, power-producing thoughts. Do this whenever a negative thought rears its ugly head. I call this *thought substitution.* At the office, at home, at the Rotary Club meeting—everywhere—whenever your thoughts drift off to the negative, stop them, then substitute positive *ki* thoughts—"I like this person." "I'm having a good time." "We can work this out." "I'm happy." "I'm going to succeed." "I'm going to win." *Always* reject negative *ki* and consciously replace it with positive.

• Spit. To add power and determination to your rejection of negative thoughts, spit out the troublesome thought. Go "thoo" and spit out the negative *ki* thought.

• Pay special attention to "red alert," negative *ki* feelings. Whenever you feel any of the following . . .

afraid, scared
confused, indecisive
distracted, upset

depressed, sad or miserable
worried, nervous, anxious, upset, tense, pressured
beaten down, defeated, your spirits sagging
listless, unmotivated and bored
shy, non-assertive, timid
defensive, ready to hit back, bitter
guilty

. . . your *ki* is negative, your *ryoku* power is weak.

Whenever you find yourself slipping into any of these feelings, immediately set off "red alert" alarms in your head. Right away, remind yourself of *shin-ki-ryoku*. Tell yourself, "Remember, transmit your *ki*." Click into a more positive frame of mind by substituting plus thoughts for minuses. If you're like most people you will feel recharged immediately.

• Control your expectations. Negative-expectations, negative *ki* people are that way only out of habit. By developing new, more positive *ki* thought habits you condition yourself to have positive expectations and you put more power into your actions.

Expect others to like you, *expect* to make the sale, *expect* to enjoy the job interview and to get the job, *expect* to be able to work out whatever business or personal problems confront you. Always jump to the positive side and expect to happen what you want to happen.

• Constantly remind yourself of the importance of positive *shin*, positive *ki*. If you work or live with someone else who knows about *ki*, form a pact. If one of you is becoming tight, irritable or gloomy, the other one is to say, "C'mon now. Don't forget. Transmit your *ki*."

Write out reminders on three-by-five index cards and put them in prominent places around your house and office. "Plus creates plus." "Good *shin* creates good *ki* creates power." Read them aloud, and with feeling, from time to time. On each card draw a large minus sign and a large plus sign. Draw an arrow from the minus to the plus to remind yourself to move your negative thoughts to positive.

You might wish to set fire to your negative *ki* thoughts. Martial artist Bruce Lee visualized his negative thoughts written on a piece of paper, then saw himself wadding the paper into a ball, lighting it with a match and watching it burn to a crisp. He said the thoughts never returned to disturb him.

• Draw a ring of harmony around yourself wherever you are. You can generate goodwill and cooperation by imagining a yellow ring of harmony around you constantly. Make the ring red or blue if you like—the color doesn't matter. All that matters is your imagining the ring around yourself and making certain that whenever another person passes into it there is cooperation and harmony between you.

• Stop judging others negatively. People can pick up very quickly if you're thinking they're dumb, nasty, unpleasant, overly talkative, ugly, poorly dressed, too highly paid for what they do, etc. If they sense that you don't like them, they won't like you. So instead, like them, respect them, find real value in them, even if you have to work hard at it.

• Be generous with your feelings. If you like people, let them know about it. Transmit your *ki* to them. Much of the negative *ki* in business is caused by the supervisor who always criticizes and never praises. Parents often do the same with their children. Simply let people know you appreciate what they're doing and morale will improve immediately—in business and in the home.

• *See* your positive *ki* being passed from you to others. Highly developed masters are able to direct a coat of *ki* to their arm and sustain a hard sword-blow without being injured. I don't suggest you try that, but you may wish to see your positive *ki* as a ray of white light being transmitted by you to another person or a whole group of people. Actually visualize it moving from you to others under the direction of your mind.

• Maintain your *ki* even in defeat. *Everyone gets beaten.* The question is not whether you'll experience defeat, but how you'll handle it when you do. Even the great samurai Musashi took it on the chin once. When you're beaten—by another person, an event, a situation—keep your *ki* positive and strong. Never let the defeat "penetrate your depths," never let it get to your *ki.* Be able to say, "I lost this one (job, person, disagreement, etc.) but I'm not defeated. I've failed, but I'm not a failure. I've still got the only weapon I need—*me.*" Even in defeat—*especially* in defeat—keep your *ki* going full blast.

2. Focus on Your One Point

"When you're afraid, tense the muscles of your stomach and the
   fear will disappear."

                                                             Zen adage

To many Orientals the center of a person's spirit and strength is a point within the abdominal cavity two inches below the navel. This special point is called the *tai ten, tanden, tan-tien, tan, seika-tanden,* or simply "the one point." In addition to being your body's center of gravity, the one point is also the center of *ki.* The one point is comparable to the boiler of a steam engine. When your mind is concentrated on it, energy is created and distributed throughout your body, and your body is able to move quickly and powerfully.

The fighter, the *bushi,* didn't discover the power of the one point, or *naiki,* the doctrine of *ki.* All he did was use the one point for its applications to battle. He followed the edict, "Whether sitting, standing or moving, you must always take care that your lower abdomen is filled with strength."

R. E. West, a powerfully built Western black belt *judoka* (practitioner of *judo)* who knew very little about *ki* and the one point, asked an old, 130-pound Japanese master for a demonstration of its power. The two men sat on their knees facing each other. Each placed his right hand on the other's chest. Hard as West tried, he couldn't budge the old man. Then the old man gave a push and West flew backward. The master then said it was only because of the power in his one point that he could knock West over.

The way to draw the power of *ki* is very easy. Just concentrate your mind fully on your one point. Look at your stomach and find the point two inches directly below your navel. Now press it hard with your finger. This will leave a residual feeling of where the one point is. Then simply visualize. Don't look at it, just imagine it as a point, a dot.

Now that you've located the one point, practice beginning your everyday actions with your attention on it until it becomes second nature to you. Before starting any task, any task at all, first think of your one point —sitting down at your desk, starting a meeting, going to a party, entering a sales conference—whatever. If you devote yourself to concentrating on your one point it will gradually become a habit. Until it does you will have to remind yourself: "Hey, concentrate on your one point."

When you're able to remember to begin at least some of your acts from the one point, become a little more ambitious. Get in the habit of concentrating on the one point when you're upset or irritated. You'll find yourself becoming calm and strong at the same time.

After you've started the habit of one-point concentration, begin to use it during times of more severe tension and nervousness. When you're going into combat against an inner or outer opponent, concentrate your mind on your one point. When you're troubled and your thoughts and emotions are shooting around like rockets, concentrate on your one point. *Whenever* you need to, simply concentrate on your one point.

If you find the idea of concentrating on your one point a little strange or you're skeptical or feel odd doing it, don't worry about it, just do it anyway. It *will* work.

3. Practice Deep, Abdominal Breathing

"If you know the art of breathing you have the strength, wisdom
and courage of ten tigers."

Chinese adage

Breathe the right way. When you do you fill yourself with *ki.* It courses through your body, exhilarating you in ways you haven't even imagined yet, and it increases the energy field around you.

The advice to breathe the right way may sound silly and even insulting. "Hell," you say, "I've been breathing all my life. I'm alive because I breathe. No one has to teach me to breathe."

And of course you're right. The problem is, however, that while the way we breathe is sufficient for most of our life-sustaining needs, it isn't sufficient to create increased supplies of *ki.*

There is breathing high and breathing low. Westerners breathe high. We are taught "stomach in, chest out." Our breathing is done high in our chest. *Ki* breathing is done low. It's bringing the inhaled air far down in the lungs. In other words, as far as *ki* development is concerned we have learned to breathe wrong. Right breathing is "chest in, stomach out." It's breathing from the abdomen—it's diaphragmatic breathing.

Deep abdominal, diaphragmatic breathing has been shown to have particular advantages over "high chest," shallow breathing. Medical researchers estimate that up to 80 percent of all diseases are attributable to nervous problems. Worry, nervousness, anger and stress narrow our capillaries and restrict the flow of blood carrying fresh oxygen. By breathing the right way, you can open your capillaries and send oxygen freely throughout your body. Diaphragmatic *ki* breathing also increases your physical strength. That's another reason why the samurai was so interested in his *sanchin,* "breathing exercises."

If you're conscientious about practicing your *ki* breathing you may come to breathe this way all the time. Most people, however, even if they don't forever after breathe in the *ki* way, use it as an alternative way of breathing. When confronted with disturbing situations, when in trouble or doubt, or when they're in need of a pick-me-up, they simply drop their normal high chest breathing and launch into deep abdominal *ki* breathing.

To prepare yourself to use *ki* breathing whenever you wish you will literally need to get the feel of how to do it. Here is an easy-to-follow process:

• Get in a comfortable, relaxed position—your weight on your legs and feet, lying on your back, or sitting comfortably.

• Concentrate your attention on your one point. Remember it's the center of gravity point located two inches below your navel. Throughout your *ki* breathing keep your mind on your one point. When your thoughts wander from it don't fight them, just think of your one point.

• Get rid of the carbon dioxide in your lungs by opening your mouth and making a slow, steady "haaa" sound as you breathe out for twenty seconds. When you think you're out of breath make one last hard "ha."

• Inhale slowly, evenly and deeply through your nose in one uninterrupted motion taking four or five seconds. Concentrate on bringing your breath far down. Imagine your diaphragm swelling out like a balloon and your breath pressing your one point from inside your stomach. Your breathing should be going on in your diaphragm and not in your chest. Your chest should be moving very little, if at all.

• Your attention still on your one point, and your breath pressing against it, hold your breath for five to ten seconds.

• Then exhale deeply, but slowly and evenly through your mouth. Consciously pull in your abdominal muscle to force out as much carbon dioxide as possible. If you get out of breath just stop and breathe in your usual way for a few seconds. Then start your *ki* breathing again.

Try to practice this method of *ki* breathing at least five minutes twice each day. If you set aside time every day for *ki* breathing you'll feel the effects of it not only when you're actually doing it, but throughout the day.

If you're like a lot of people and twice a day is asking a lot, at least learn how to do your breathing so you can launch into it when you're upset or unsettled, or when you just feel like it.

It doesn't take long to get the hang of it and once you do you can do it whenever you wish. When your *ki* is lively, you react confidently and quickly. If it's clouded and negative, you hesitate and become awkward and indecisive. Therefore, keep your *ki* flowing all day long.

After you have become accustomed to deep abdominal *ki* breathing you can do it anywhere—in a cab, on a train, at your desk, while walking down the street, in an elevator. *Whenever* you need *ki* simply breathe down to your one point.

Points to Remember: Ki: The Spirit of the Warrior

• Remember to do what the chapter asks you to—"Fill yourself with *ki.*" Do it as often as you can. In particular, do it to increase your expectations of success and whenever you experience defeat.

• *Ki* is energy, a frame of mind or attitude, and it's a force that you communicate to other people.

• Positive *ki* creates positive power in your actions and positive responses in others. Negative *ki* creates negative actions and responses.

• Make certain you never forget the personal power formula of *shin-ki-ryoku.* Your frame of mind determines how much energy you have and the amount of power you live and work with. You can choose how much power you will communicate by choosing what to think.

• To increase your *ki* and *ryoku* power, apply the three samurai steps of (1) transmitting your *ki,* (2) concentrating on your one point two inches below your navel and (3) breathing diaphragmatically.

• The time will come when you realize you have been neglecting your *ki* development. Whenever that happens, go back to this chapter and refresh your memory of how you can increase your *ki* and *ryoku* power whenever you want to.

5

Developing *Joriki,* Your Power of Concentration in Action

"The focused mind can pierce through stone."
Japanese maxim

Centuries ago there lived a man who had devoted himself completely to *kyudo,* the Way of the bow. Early one evening he was walking in the mountains when suddenly he saw a flicker of movement in the shadows. It was a tiger, its back arched, ready to pounce. Without hesitation the archer nocked the arrow. Concentrating all his power in the shot, since it might be his last, he let the arrow fly. A direct hit, right in the head. Without stopping to examine the dead animal, the archer continued on his way.

The next day, though, he became curious and returned to the spot. But hard as he looked he could not find the dead animal. He was about to abandon his search when he saw the arrow, stuck in a huge boulder. It hadn't been a tiger after all, but his concentration had been so intense and his shot so powerful that the arrow had been driven into solid rock.

From this incident came the famous maxim about concentration and power in any Way of life: *"Ichinen iwa wo mo tosu,"* "The focused mind can pierce through stone."

Your Stones Are There for the Piercing

"Concentration. You've got to concentrate."
O. J. Simpson

"The focused mind can pierce through stone" is not a dramatic exaggeration. It's literally true. Hou Shuying of Peking, China, is a fifty-year-old exponent of *qigong*, a "breaking art" that teaches the development of almost unbelievable power through mental concentration. Hou not only can break stones and wood but can snap iron bars in two by chopping them with his bare hands. In a recent demonstration he broke a four-inch-thick slab of granite in half with a sharp blow with his head!

Mas Oyama, considered by many the greatest contemporary martial artist, brought down a full-grown charging bull with two blows. The first sliced one of the bull's horns in half and the second caught the animal on the head and dropped him.

With one fingertip, martial artists can punch a hole in a coconut. One night karate master Itosu was awakened by noises at the wooden front gate of his home. From the sounds, he could tell that someone was trying to pick the lock. With one blow he punched a hole in the thick wood and seized the wrist of the would-be burglar. The hole was perfectly round; there had been no shattering.

Joriki. "The power of concentration." It has nothing to do with muscle and brawn. It's not visible to the eye. Read the maxim again and notice that it was the archer's *mind* that pierced the boulder. Focus your mind on whatever you're doing, from letting arrows fly to doing business or living at the gut level, and your arrows will penetrate.

Studies of materially successful people reveal that they operate the way that archer and the "breaking" artists did. They have complete faith in the rightness of their decisions and they follow through on them with a focused, stone-piercing concentration.

Right now think of a task that's ahead of you, any task at all . . . .

Whatever you thought of, you will handle it best when—like that archer—you focus your mind on it 100 percent, excluding everything else. Writing a report, conducting a meeting, pursuing your bottom-line life goals, solving a personal or business problem, making more money, selling a product, out-competing the competition, crossing swords with a dreaded enemy, sinking a putt . . . these are just a few sample tasks, a few stones that are ready for piercing.

So why aren't you piercing more of your stones? It's those . . .

. . . Damned Drunken Monkeys

In the Orient, everyday awareness has been compared to a drunken monkey. Our thoughts stagger around like a monkey that's been hitting the sauce.

Give your mind a sobriety test. Just sit back and listen to your thoughts. Unless you're already a high *joriki* concentrator you'll probably notice that your mind bounces drunkenly from one thing to another. One moment you're thinking about the job at hand, then about how hungry you are or another task you've got to do or the score of a ball game, or of sex, or how boring the job is or how difficult, or that tennis elbow pain that's acting up.

Those are moment-to-moment drunken monkeys. There is another kind, one that can come to dominate the course of a person's life.

Some people will tell you that the thing they *really* want to accomplish in their lives is . . . to be rich . . . write a novel . . . run a successful business . . . find a satisfying job . . . etc. But even as they're telling you, you know they will never do it. Why? One reason—one of the biggest—is because inside their heads they're staggering around from one goal to another, one possibility to another, without rhyme or reason or conscious direction. They're letting the drunken monkeys guide them. Is it any wonder that they are ending up miles from where they say they want to be?

Many companies, too, have drunken monkeys in their corporate heads. In *Managing for Results,* consultant and author Peter Drucker states that "No other principle of effectiveness is violated as constantly today as the basic principle of concentration." The motto of business (and government and big universities, for that matter) seems to be "Let's do a little bit of everything." The result, says Drucker, is that "we build enormous staffs, and yet do not concentrate enough effort in any one area."

To remedy this, he believes that managers must learn to concentrate their efforts, focusing on the smallest possible number of products, markets and customers that will produce the largest profits.

Life comes at you point blank—problems, tasks, responsibilities and decisions. You could cry out, "Hold it, life, I'm not ready yet," but that's not going to gain you anything. When ten men are attacking you, says sword master Takuan, as soon as one is disposed of, you must move on to another and focus on disposing of him. You shouldn't have problems if you concentrate, but if you can't, if your head monkeys are drunk, you're in trouble.

Concepts of Concentration

1. *Shuchu-ryoku*

Shuchu-ryoku is the ability to concentrate all of your mental and muscular power at a given instant at one particular focal point. It's concentrating all the power you've got on one task, one goal, one problem or one object at a time.

Karate experts have won arm wrestling contests using only their little finger. They claim that they were really at an advantage since using only one finger enabled them to concentrate their full strength in only one small area. Applying *shuchu-ryoku*, if the martial artist is launching a blow with his right hand he puts no strength in his left, for this would reduce the power in his right.

Put it this way: if you (or a corporation) possess one hundred units of energy and expend ten units each on handling ten problems, you might not be able to handle one problem that requires ninety units to solve. But if you're able to concentrate all one hundred units on one problem after another, *shuchu-ryoku* style, you can solve them.

2. *Seiryoku Zenryo*

Just watch a master in any field—the master talk-show hosts Johnny Carson and Phil Donahue; or the best businessman you ever met; or your friend Sally, who is able to accomplish so much you're jealous.

You'll notice one quality immediately. It's a finesse, a grace, an ease, a relaxed effortlessness. They make the performance look easy.

What they're displaying is one of the principal concepts of *budo,* the Way of the samurai. It's *seiryoku zenryo,* or *maximum efficiency with minimum effort.* It's the economical use of energy of any kind, mental or physical. If you're a business manager and you think for a while about *seiryoku zenryo,* maximum efficiency with minimum effort, eventually you will have a eureka insight, and you will be exactly right. Yes, it's the precise definition of high productivity. If your entire work force were to operate *seiryoku zenryo,* you would be making full output use of your labor.

And it pertains not only to physical energy, but to emotional energy too. Most of us dissipate much of our energy in unnecessarily fretting, hating, being afraid, becoming impatient and annoyed and in enduring all the other strength-sapping feelings. We're only robbing ourselves of the strength we need to face and solve our problems. Once you are able to divert energy from those emotions and to pour it into achieving goals, your power is boundless.

3. *Kufu*

I was interviewing people for a job that required the ability to write reports. While he wanted the job, Jack confided that he had a problem —writer's block. Anyone who will apply for a writer's job and be so honest as to tell the person doing the hiring that he has problems writing is my kind of guy.

He told me more. "When I sit down to work, all that I want to say seems clear to me. But when I actually start I have a tough time. The ideas and words don't come. I try, but after about an hour I give up. I've even stopped writing completely. What do you think I should do?"

"Don't quit after an hour," I said.

The point I was making was a simple samurai one. I was telling Jack to *kufu* his way out.

Kufu. It's a wonderful concept that applies equally to the small everyday tasks and problems in your life and to the big ones too. It means giving yourself completely to discovering the solution or to finding the way out of your difficulties and to your objective. It means to struggle, to grapple, to wrestle until you find the way out. It is holding nothing back, but giving your all. It is closing ground on the problem and never retreating or hanging back. With *kufu* the problem is your opponent. To defeat it you advance on it with all you've got, again and again, until you come out victorious.

When you take the *kufu*, grapple-your-way-out approach, you know that somewhere ahead of you lies a breakthrough point, a moment when you will get the better of the problem or the task. It is there awaiting you. All you have to do is remain concentrated on the battle long enough to reach it.

"Who knows," I told Jack, "but your breakthrough point could come at sixty-one minutes or seventy-five or four thousand. If you give up after an hour you'll never reach it. *Kufu* your way out of this writer's block."

Months later Jack returned to tell me that he had gone back to his writing to try the *kufu* approach of staying with it, trying it again and again, no matter how long it took. Suddenly, he said, writing had become not totally effortless, but noticeably less effortful.

No one is spared resistances to the breakthrough experience. Jack continued to encounter concentration blocks from time to time, but he had learned what many people never learn: the *kufu* spirit of staying with it until you win.

Four Drunken Monkeys and How to Overcome Them

"When attacking, don't be careless."
The Way of the spear

All drunken monkeys in your head—your individual head or your corporate head—are blocks to *joriki*, concentration power. They are inner dragons that interfere with *shuchu-ryoku* (one-point concentration), *seiryoku zenryo* (maximum efficiency), and *kufu* (problem-solving). To say that a person or an organization is not highly concentrated is another way of saying that they are expending too much energy on blocks and not enough on goals and tasks.

Below are four commonly encountered "drunken monkey" blocks to *joriki* concentration power. While they can affect one's personal life, they're particularly prevalent in business.

• *The ball-juggling block.* Trying to juggle too many balls (goals, tasks, activities) at the same time.

• *The boredom block.* If you find yourself thinking, "Life is supposed to be exciting, so why is my job so dull?" you might be suffering from the Boredom Block.

• *The perceived-difficulty block.* It's looking at what you have to do and thinking, "Lord above, this job is just too hard for me," and letting the apparent difficulty drive you into the surrender of inaction.

• *The domination-of-deadlines block.* Deadlines are supposed to facilitate the timely completion of work. When the deadline becomes an intimidator instead of a facilitator, you're up against the Domination of Deadlines Block.

Following is a description of each of these four blocks and tips for overcoming them.

The Ball-Juggling Block

> "Among your affairs there should be no more than two or three
> matters of great concern."
>
> *Hagakure*

I remember flying to a large midwestern city for an early morning breakfast meeting with three executives of one of the world's largest corporations. As I forked into the plump yolks of my eggs, the conversation turned to how busy they all were.

"Right now," said an exhausted Sam, who was late for the meeting and came in huffing, "I'm juggling twenty balls at the same time."

"Hell," Bob replied, "twenty is nothing. I've got thirty, thirty-five up there."

"Chicken feed," chimed in Vern. He went on to estimate the extraordinary number of projects he was trying to oversee.

If a man is a juggler one thing he probably is *not* is a *shuchu-ryoku*, a one-focal-point concentrator. And he's more than likely got his *seiryoku zenryo* backwards—putting out maximum effort and yielding minimum efficiency. Given all the juggling going on, and the pride attached to it, is it surprising to find stress and burnout on the rise, and efficiency plummeting?

During that breakfast meeting I was reminded of one of the stories about concentration from the Way of the archer. The greatest bowmen in the land were invited to a contest. A fish was put up a pole a great distance away. Asked by the judge if they could see the fish, one by one the archers said they could. One last contestant stepped to the line

"Can you see the fish?" asked the judge.

The archer replied, "I'm looking at its eye."

This was the champion.

Learn to concentrate on the fish's eye in whatever you're shooting at and you'll win more often than not.

The lack of organizational concentration creates ball-juggling bigness —departmentalization, division of labor, complexity; these in turn create conflicts between departments and confusions about end-purposes, thus reducing *seiryoku zenryo*, maximum efficiency.

Tips for Handling the Ball-Juggling Block

The following tips can be used by individuals or whole companies:

• If you're in business, think small. Pare down, whittle away, reduce the number of balls you're trying to juggle and narrow your focus. Master the art of keeping things small and you also master the art of concentration. Economy of movement, *mo chih ch'u*—leaping into action—was vital to the samurai. It is the ability to move quickly time and again—to spend less time between idea and implementation—that separates the smaller, sleeker business from the larger ones.

Futurist Alvin Toffler has correctly observed that many organizations are realizing they have exceeded the limits of the economics of scale. They're just too big. The alternative is for companies to increase efficiency by finding ways to make their work units smaller—forgetting about the fish and shooting only at its eye.

Matsushita, manufacturers of National, Panasonic, Technics and Quasar brands, is a huge Japanese corporation employing two hundred thousand people. To assure smallness, even amidst bigness, Matsushita decentralizes responsibility and authority outward from its headquarters to its smaller divisions, each of which is expected to operate like a small, fast-on-its-feet company.

• If you're already small, concentrate even more. The U.S. Department of Labor estimates that three quarters of the new jobs in this country over the last decade were created among the relatively small employers. There is business growth in the United States, and it is occurring among the smaller, highly concentrated companies.

• Whether you're a big business or a small one, emphasize *shuchuryoku*, full power directed at a narrow focal point. Why disperse your firm's resources trying to sell fourteen services fairly well for one million dollars when chances are you would make more than a million—and perhaps far more—if you concentrated your resources on selling seven services superbly well?

• Whether you work in a big company or a small one, put *seiryoku zenryo*, "maximum efficiency with minimum effort," into your work. If you're a salesman, instead of spending three months of hard work and aggravation on making a fifty-thousand-dollar sale, devote the same time and toil to another prospect that will bring in twice that amount. Just recognize what your own experience tells you: to close a ten-thousand-dollar sale does not require ten times the effort of making a one-thousand-dollar sale. Generally, they take about the same.

• Whatever your business is, take an inventory of the balls you're currently juggling. Take out a sheet of paper and list all the goals, activities, projects and tasks that are vying for your attention.

• Prepare a list of the few balls you *should* be juggling. *Hagakure*, the guide for samurai, says, "Among your affairs there should be no more than two or three matters of great concern." Those "matters of great concern" are the balls you *must* keep going. Sift through the list and even if each one seems to be saying to you, "Do me," force yourself to select only the two or three that are of great concern.

• Find opportunities to intentionally drop one less important ball after another. The less important balls are the ones that have been diverting you from the really important pursuits and pleasures in your life —from the two or three balls that are of great concern, that really count. Matters of great concern are the goals and tasks that you feel you *must* pursue and can no longer sacrifice.

• Whatever you find yourself (or your business) doing, ask if at that moment it is contributing to your two or three matters of great concern. If it isn't, don't do it, or at least seriously consider not doing it. But if it is, concentrate on it *shuchu-ryoku*—with all your attention and energy.

The Boredom Block

Iaido is the art of drawing a long sword *(katana)*, making a few cuts or thrusts, and returning the sword to the scabbard—all with lightning speed. Want to know how skilled an *iaidoka* is? All you have to do is check his *koiguchi*, the open slot of his scabbard. If it's not scratched, he's a master. That's concentration.

You might find it hard to imagine anything more boring than whipping a sword from a scabbard only to return it again, and doing this devotedly tens of thousands of times. But that's the point. Boredom is only a drunken-monkey belief that there is something else you would rather be doing. Get rid of that belief and you'll get rid of boredom.

Tips for Handling the Boredom Block

• Find something of interest in the "boring" task. Give more of your attention to something and it will become more interesting. And the more interesting it becomes the more attention you'll want to give to it.

The famous naturalist Agassiz was known for turning out students with highly developed powers of observation. Many of them went on to become eminent in the field.

A new student appeared and asked Agassiz to teach him. Agassiz took a fish from the jar of preservative and said, "Observe this fish carefully and when I return be ready to report to me what you noticed."

Left alone, the student sat down to look at the fish. It was a fish just like any other. The student finished looking and sat waiting, but no teacher. Hours passed and the student grew restless. He asked himself why he had hooked up with an old man who was obviously behind the times.

With nothing else to do, the student counted the scales, then the spines of the fins, then drew a picture of the fish. In doing so, he noticed the fish had no eyelids. He continued drawing and noticing other things that had escaped him. And he learned that even a fish is interesting if you really see it.*

• Listen. If certain people bore you, it could be because you're not hearing them. Drop your assessment that the speaker is boring and listen. You might be surprised to discover how much there is to that person.

• Make up interest-inducing statements for yourself. If you persist in telling yourself something is boring, that's just how you'll find it. But silence such thoughts as "This is boring" and replace them with "There is something stimulating here. All I've got to do is find it," and you'll be surprised how interesting things can be.

• Tackle the most interesting part of the job first. Most tasks have features that you find boring and others that you find more interesting. Bodybuilders often start their workouts with lifts they enjoy most. Once started, they go on to the lifts they enjoy less. Try to do the same whatever you're lifting.

• Change your routine. Sometimes it's not the tasks that are boring, but the routine of carrying them out. Change your schedule. Take a different route to work. Do on Wednesday what you always do on Monday. Stand up when you talk on the phone instead of sitting down, etc.

• Set up periodic pick-me-up projects for yourself. Working on new projects is a wonderful way to ward off boredom.

• Stay physically active. Hit golf balls or get down on the floor and do some push-ups. One of the least bored men I ever met had a set of dumbbells in his office closet. Whenever he found himself thinking "This is bo-o-o-o-ring" he did twenty curls.

* Ramacharaka, *Raja Yoga* (Bombay, 1966).

Shinichi Suzuki, developer of the Suzuki method of music instruction, was invited to a factory to give a talk to its workers. Afterwards, the director of the company told Suzuki that the factory employed about thirty people who worked very slowly.

Suzuki recommended that the workers be allowed to play ping-pong for one hour each day during working hours, and that the company hire a coach to teach them. A year later Suzuki received a glowing letter, stating that the director had implemented the suggestion and that the workers' efficiency had improved unbelievably.

• Take breaks. Working hard in short, intense, concentrated spurts, with rest periods between spurts, is turning out to be the best way to work in many fields.

• Alter the content of your life or work. Let's say you have tried like the devil to find something interesting in the "boring" task, tried to see things freshly, etc. You have even taken off a few weeks and gone to Hawaii, and you have returned to find the same boredom in your life or work—big-*B* Boredom. If so, identify the specific aspects of your life/ work situation that bore you, and consider slicing them off like shavings off a stick.

The Perceived-Difficulty Block

Do you ever look at the task ahead of you and find yourself thinking, "I don't get it," or "It's too damned complicated," or "I'll never be able to do this?" If so, you've come nose to nose with the *perceived-difficulty block*. It's an imposing block to maximum efficiency with minimum effort—*seiryoku zenryo*. And it accounts for many failures to complete work—from repairing a leaky drainpipe to realizing important life goals.

Tips for Dealing with the Perceived-Difficulty Block

• Recognize that work of every kind is a performance you can learn— if you're patient.

Let's admit it, *kufu*—grappling with something until we master it—doesn't come easy for most Americans. We have a TV-rating kind of mentality. It's either quick results or cancellation. It's the same with many of our efforts in business and personal life—a couple of tries without reaching success and it's ratings time again: "Who needs this noise? I'm canceling out."

A few years ago playing tennis was all the rage. Slews of people rushed out, bought expensive clothes and equipment and joined tennis clubs. The tennis business boomed. It was the right racket to be in. But then just as suddenly it began to decline. Why? Because many a consumer of tennis products suddenly realized that having the equipment, the clothes and the membership did not in any way assure one of the ability to play a decent game of tennis. Playing a decent game meant trying and failing and trying again. It meant hard work and sweat.

Ratings time again. The equipment and clothes were packed away and the membership was allowed to lapse.

Right now you have a virtually limitless capacity to learn to do just about anything—but only if you're willing to put out the effort. Learn to look past the surface *seiryoku zenryo* ease of the master; see the effort and devotion that went into creating it, and then . . .

• *Kufu* your way to victory. Look around and see the victors. Is it a special gift or talent that brought them success? Usually not. How many times have you heard of someone you know achieving great success and thought something like—"Bill a multimillionaire real-estate genius? Back in high school he couldn't hold a candle to me. Are you sure it's Bill you're talking about?"

It's Bill all right—or Mary, as the case may be. There's nothing special about their innate ability, but look them up and you'll find that they're the kind of person who, no matter what block appears, refuses to be stopped by it. They concentrate, they pierce stones, they *kufu* their way to victory.

• Counterattack all self-blaming put-downs. When your mind starts playing games, with its "This should be easy," or "Charley does this kind of thing so easily" or "Maybe I wasn't meant to be a . . . (public speaker, manager, salesman)" kinds of thoughts, don't let it get away with it. Who says anything should be easy? Does Charley really do it so easily or are you just not aware of the sweat and toil he puts in?

And even if he does it with ease while you have to struggle, so what?

Concentrate on your own game, not your opponent's. Even if you're a tortoise and things don't come easily to you and the Charleys of the world are hares, stay with it. Play your own game. The world's full of loser hares and winner tortoises.

• Recognize that your imagination often makes the task seem more difficult than it really is. Often difficulty is only something you imagine. In reality the task usually turns out to be easier than you thought.

• Consciously change your thinking. Change it from "This is too hard for me" to "The best way out is through."

• Get started! At times people and businesses are intimidated by the enormity of the task that lies before them. They look at where they are and where they want to be, and the sometimes tremendous gulf between the two can be very discouraging. "I'm here now and I want to get *way* over there. Wow!" The longer you sit back and worry, the more awesome and intimidating the work becomes. Instead, seize the offensive and leap forward now. Leaping forward *now* is fighting like a samurai.

• Reduce the big task into smaller segments. Select one small part of the whole task and begin working on it. Say to yourself, "Little by little, I'll just *shuchu-ryoku* my way through this," and do it.

• Rather than fretting or spending far too much time on a task or project that's beyond your abilities at the time, get help. The more successful business operator is the one who makes use of experts and specialized personnel. It's ridiculous to try to do everything yourself. Make use of skilled resources. That's maximum efficiency with minimum effort.

The Domination-of-Deadlines Block

"I'll never finish on time. My butt's in a sling."
Anonymous businessman

Theoretically, due-date deadlines are there to aid our concentration. While they're supposed to help concentration, and often do, deadlines can easily become drunken-monkey blocks. Just think how ominous the word "deadline" is. It is not a *life*line but a *dead*line.

Let's say that once into the work you encounter a snag. The internal voice begins: "You're falling behind. You might not finish on time." Your mind begins to conjure up a grim chain of consequences: "If I don't finish on time the estimate won't go out. If it doesn't go out we'll lose the sale. If we lose the sale I'll lose my job. If I lose my job . . ." The more you worry about the deadline, the more time passes and the more you find yourself in a time bind. "Oh, God, no matter what, I can't possibly finish on time now."

Tips on Handling
the Deadline Block

• Learn to set realistic time estimates by using "the kick." Early in my career I was extremely optimistic in my time estimates. My staff and I would meet the deadline, but always at some cost. I recall having an entire office working in pain and discomfort with serious cases of the flu simply because of my unrealistic estimate.

I developed a simple technique which I called "the kick." It consisted of one of my associates kicking me under the table when a client asked me to name the completion date. The kick was a signal for me to double my estimate.

I have an engineer friend who lost six jobs because of his unrealistic time estimates. I told him about "the kick" and suggested that he use it. He did, and it saved his job.

• Realize that a *realistic* deadline is a positive motivator to action. Research has shown that some pressure actually enhances the performance. The great majority of athletes perform better in the game than in practice simply because of the added pressure.

• Pay no attention to the deadline. The key to ridding yourself of any block to concentration is to refuse to let your attention waver from the work itself.

Archery contests are held at a temple in Kyoto. Its west veranda is 128 yards long. Since its ceiling is low, the archer has to shoot without much arch, a feat requiring considerable strength. The idea is to see how many arrows can be shot from one end of the veranda to the other in a day. The record is 8,133, or about five arrows each minute for twenty-four consecutive hours. How many arrows would have been shot had the archer stopped to worry and fret about the twenty-four-hour deadline? Certainly not 8,133.

Resist any inclination to worry about the deadline. Don't worry, just shoot your arrows. You will meet your deadlines and produce better-quality work to the degree that you forget about the deadline and shift your concentration entirely to the work.

• Use thought-replacement. You can think whatever you want to whenever you want to. For every "Oh, hell, I'm falling behind again" thought, replace it with "I'm whittling this job down," or with "Every time I stop to tell myself I'm not making it I'm losing time."

Being Mindful: An All-Purpose Method for Overcoming Blocks to Joriki

When you're "mindful" you act deliberately, you mean to act the way you do, you put your intention into the act. Whenever you do something because you have consciously intended to do it, immediately there is more power in your actions.

• At the start of the day promise that whatever you do during the next twenty-four hours you're going to try to concentrate on it, you're going to mean to do it.

• Make moment-by-moment decisions to concentrate. Whatever is facing you, say to yourself, "At this moment I'm going to do this thing and only it."

• When you notice a concentration block creeping in to divert your attention, *intend* that much more.

For example . . .

. . . you sit down to work and suddenly you think of another ball you could be juggling, or . . .

. . . you're preparing to speak to a group of people and the perceived-difficulty block makes you scared. Pea-sized beads of sweat pop out on your forehead . . .

Tell yourself, "There's a block here. I could let it suck me in and divert me but I won't. I *want* to do the task at hand; I *will* do it."

Don't try to force yourself not to be blocked. Force won't work here. Have you ever tried to force yourself not to hear the dripping faucet?

Sure, and the *only* thing you could hear after that was the damn dripping!

Just forget about the block and think only of what you have to do. Whenever your mind drifts back to the block don't fight it, just withdraw your attention by nudging it back again to the job at hand.

• Constantly remind yourself of the importance of the task. In themselves, most everyday and business tasks seem like little, mundane, meaningless chores. An "80–20" principle in management is that 80 percent of your job satisfaction derives from 20 percent of the tasks you perform. But the moment you see that the remaining 80 percent—the "dull" tasks—are necessary steps to achieve something larger and more important, your concentration increases, at times phenomenally.

You can do this by consciously giving each task a larger significance. Again and again return to your *bushido*, your bottom-line purpose. Put whatever you do in the context of serving that *bushido*. Do that and no act is ever a dull chore.

Going to the drugstore may seem like a boring thing to do, but going there to buy medicine for your sick child is an act of love. Same act, but a different meaning—a *bushido* meaning.

If you're an auditor, putting on your green eyeshade and adding a column of figures may seem dull, but remind yourself that you are doing it to serve your purpose of making money for your family and what was drudgery a moment ago takes on a *bushido* meaning. *Mokuteki hon'i*, "focus on your purpose." Get in the habit of saying it to yourself ten, fifteen or thirty times a day.

Points to Remember: Developing Joriki, Your Power of Concentration in Action

• "The focused mind can pierce through stone." It's worth remembering.

• *Joriki*, "the power of concentration," is internal. Concentrate and your arrows *will* penetrate. Don't take my word for it. Concentrate and you'll show yourself.

• *Shuchu-ryoku*—the ability to concentrate all your energy, muscular and mental, at one focal point.

• *Seiryoku zenryo*, or "maximum efficiency with minimum effort." It's high productivity in any area of your life.

• *Kufu*. It means to grapple and struggle with a problem, task or difficulty until you find the way out, the breakthrough point. Whenever a grim opponent is facing you—out there or inside you—tell yourself, "I've got to *kufu* my way out of this thing."

• Ball-juggling, boredom, perceived difficulty and the domination of deadlines are four serious blocks to *joriki*, concentration power. Learn to recognize these blocks when you encounter them, then apply the tips for overcoming them which this chapter provides.

• Being mindful is acting deliberately, intentionally. Learn the method of mindfulness and whatever your work or personal life calls on you to do, you'll do it with concentration.

6

Reaching *Mushin,* the Samurai Alternative

"When all psychological blocks are removed . . . the swordsman will move without conscious effort."

Sword master Muneyoshi Yagyu (1527–1606)

The Storekeeper and the Thief

In Japan in the last century, storekeepers were considered lily-livered weaklings. One storekeeper became sick and tired of this reputation. To prove that it was totally false he took lessons at a martial arts *dojo.* He devoted himself religiously and after some years he became an expert.

After closing his shop late one night, the storekeeper and his wife started home down the dark streets. They had just turned the corner when a man holding a knife stepped out of the shadows and ordered the storekeeper to hand over his money.

At first he refused, but when the thief charged him, growling, "You miserable merchant, I'll cut you to pieces," the storekeeper lost his courage, fell to his knees, and began to tremble with fear.

Suddenly his wife cried out, "You're not a storekeeper, you're an expert in the martial arts."

The storekeeper turned his head and looked at his wife. "Yes," he said, "I am."

He stood, a warrior now, totally fearless, completely calm. He let out a powerful *katzu,* "battle shout," and leaped at the thief. He defeated him easily in a matter of seconds.

The Teaman and the Ronin

In feudal Japan, a poor practitioner of *chado,* the Way of tea, unwittingly insulted a *ronin,* a masterless samurai. Outraged, the ronin challenged the servant to a duel.

"I'm not a warrior," the teaman said, "and I'm very sorry if I offended you. I certainly didn't mean to. Please accept my apology."

But the ronin would have none of it. "We meet at dawn tomorrow," he said, and as was customary he handed the terrified teaman a sword. "Go practice," said the ronin.

The servant ran to the home of a famous sword master and told him the terrible thing that had happened.

"A unique situation," the sword master said. "For you will surely die. The thing I might be able to help you with is *isagi-yoku,* the art of dying well."

While they talked, the teaman prepared and poured tea. The masterful way he did it caught the eye of the sword master. He slapped his knee and said, "Forget what I just told you. Put yourself into the state of mind you were in as you prepared the tea and you can win this fight."

The teaman was shocked. The sword the ronin had given him was the first he had ever held. "What state of mind?"

"Were you thinking 'I'm a teaman?' " asked the master.

"No. I wasn't thinking at all."

"That's it!" The sword master laughed. "Tomorrow draw your sword and hold it high over your head, ready to cut your opponent down. Don't think you're a teaman or that you're a swordsman. Just listen. When you hear him shout, strike him down."

The next morning the ronin appeared on the field and the teaman immediately raised his sword overhead, his eyes on the ronin, his ears waiting for the battle cry.

For long moments the ronin stared at the raised sword, and the determination in his opponent's eyes. Finally the ronin said, "I cannot beat you." He bowed to his opponent and then left the field.

The Main Event

The problem of these two men should seem familiar. Their predicament is one we all encounter every day. Our opponents aren't usually thieves and they certainly aren't wandering samurai ronin, but that's not important. Those weren't the main opponents anyway.

The primary battle, the main event, was going on inside the storekeeper and the teaman. To win on the outside, each had first to come to terms with an inner opponent, a powerful dragon.

Nowadays we call it by assorted names—self-concept, self-image, self-estimate. It's your internal, private opinion of the kind of person you are and of the actions you are or are not capable of performing. It directly controls how successful you are in fighting your personal and business battles and how full and enjoyable your life is.

"Don't Get Caught out of Your Unit"

Some years ago I consulted with a nose-to-the-grindstone organization that had a rule that no one from one unit was to visit another unit during working hours. Wherever you went you heard people saying, "Don't get caught out of your unit."

Your self-concept is like that rule. It says, "Whatever you do, don't get caught out of your self-concept." It says it all day long, every day, and in doing so it restricts your fighting ability.

It is continually telling you to stay inside its definition of *the kind of person you are* . . .

• "You're a sensitive person, so act sensitively. If you don't, shame on you, feel guilty."

• "You're the kind of person who has things under control. Oops, you lost control. Well you're going to have to suffer for it. I think I'll make you feel remorse."

• "You're an effective manager in a big corporation, but you're for the birds at running your own business."

• "Talking to people face to face—that's your strength. But woe betide you if you try to sell over the telephone."

• "You're clumsy. Go through life stumbling around."

• "You're just a teaman. There's no way you can defeat a ronin in combat."

Stick to your unit and there's a whole huge world outside you'll never get a chance to visit.

• Some people tell themselves they're losers, and because of it they go through life consistently losing fights, friends, money and opportunities. Stick to a loser unit and by definition you can't win.

Other people will tell you, "I'm not very good at getting to know strangers," or "I'm not a fighter . . . a good listener . . . good at math . . . the leader type . . . very thoughtful . . . studious . . . friendly and outgoing . . . a risk-taker," etc.

And they say, "I can't sell . . . make a lot of money . . . get to appointments on time . . . save money . . . make the big deal . . . compete with younger people at the office," and so on.

Many people have such narrow self-concepts they're living in a unit that's only a fraction of the size of their true ability. They possess the capacity to defeat thieves and ronin any time they wish, but they don't realize they do. Some people—maybe you know a few of them—have self-concepts so narrow and confining they can hardly do anything.

If your self-concept is right for you—if you're happy with it—by all means keep it. But if it's bringing you defeat, if you're dissatisfied with it, you may wish to (1) change it, or (2) operate without it.

"I'm a Warrior, Not a Storekeeper:" Changing Your Self-Concept

"Let your mind be free to function according to its own nature."
Samurai teacher

One method for releasing yourself from a self-concept that's too limiting is the one illustrated by the story of the storekeeper. The *storekeeper option* means that you replace the restricting self-concept ("I'm a cowardly storekeeper") with a more useful one, one that enables you to win more of your battles ("I'm not a lily-livered storekeeper, I'm a warrior.")

In and out of business, this type of storekeeper-to-warrior rapid change of self-concept is bringing people to a new view of themselves, to a this-

is-the-real-me illumination. For some, all it takes is a particular insight—
namely:

All self-concepts are made up.

Self-concepts are fictions. They are not real in the way a flower pot is
real or a desk is. They are merely ways you have chosen to view yourself.
From this insight it's a short, leaping step to the next: "Hey, since I
made up this damned self-concept and it's holding me back, all I have to
do to increase my possibilities is to create another one."

A salesman heard about the storekeeper and the thief and realized
immediately that he was acting like a storekeeper when all along he had
the potential to be a warrior. He experienced a sudden illumination, a
kotsunen nenki, and he came out changed.

He analyzed his sales performance and found that his per-customer
sale averaged about two thousand dollars. Why? Because, as he put it, "I
was believing I was a two-thousand-bucks-a-shot salesman." When he
upped the "price" of his self-estimate and said, "I'm not a two-thousand-
dollar-a-shot guy anymore; now I'm a twenty-thousand-dollar-a-shot
guy," he soon started making twenty-thousand-dollar sales!

Watch Your Tongue; Your Thoughts Too

Many of us are overlooking our abilities. We persist in thinking we're
storekeepers when if we just thought differently about ourselves we
would see what warriors we are.

Many business people tell themselves they're not creative. They realize that creativity is a vital element of business, particularly its leadership, but they claim they just don't have it. Yet researchers have demonstrated that as soon as people start thinking "I am creative" instead of
"I'm not creative," creativity increases, even in a matter of minutes.

Listen to the things you say about yourself and think about yourself
that begin with "I am," "I'm not," and "I can't." They are your self-
concept in action. And they directly control what is possible for you.

Hank, a middle-level executive, sits in his office complaining that less capable people are leapfrogging over him to high-paying jobs. Ask him what the problem is and he'll tell you, "I'm no good at political infighting." In fact, Hank's as clever as hell and has the mind of a marvelous strategist. Here is a potential warrior who persists in telling himself he's a storekeeper.

Robin tells herself, "Ah, I lack willpower. I just can't stick to a diet." And because of it she has real problems losing weight.

Jim will tell you he's socially awkward, is no good at small talk and hates parties. And because he tells himself the very same thing, he's exactly right.

People are what they are because they keep telling themselves they are. If they stop telling themselves they are, they change.

If people say to you, "I just can't talk in front of large groups," or "I'm not the sales type," or "I'm not a sensitive person," and then ask you if there is anything they can do about it, you might suggest that they never, *never* say that again. Then suggest they counter every "I'm not" or "I just can't" with a firm "I am" or "I can."

Saying it isn't enough. The maxim "To know and to do are one and the same thing" means that what's in your head doesn't count for anything unless you translate it into action, "body knowledge," *taiken.*

It's not enough to think, "Hey, I'm not just a storekeeper, I'm really a warrior after all." To defeat the thief you have to fight.

It may be that you're weary of your current "I'm a timid person" self-concept and you wish to be bolder. Why not try the behavior on for size? All behavior is nothing more than an act, a performance. Act the way a bold person acts and you *are* bold. Act the way a political infighter acts and you are one. Do this for every "I can't" and "I'm not" and you will see that you can and you are.

Find a model, someone who does well what you would like to do. Watch how he does it, then do it the same way yourself. Many people know how to drive before ever sitting behind a wheel because they have watched others doing it. It is said that Musashi, the "sword saint," never took a lesson; he just watched masters and imitated them.

Or borrow a little from a number of models. Tsunetomo Yamamoto, the samurai author of *Hagakure,* complained that there were no models for the perfect samurai in his day. He advised that the would-be warrior should *make* a composite model by looking at many samurai and choosing the best features from each.

Choosing the Samurai Alternative: Operating Without a Self-Concept

"Forget about death, forget about the enemy, forget about yourself; keep your thoughts motionless."

Shissai

The sword master advised the teaman, "Tomorrow draw your sword and hold it high over your head, ready to cut your opponent down. Don't think you're a teaman or that you're a swordsman. Just listen. When you hear him shout, strike him down."

In sales training sessions I often use a simple role-playing exercise that's designed to demonstrate the *samurai alternative.* The samurai alternative is *not* replacing your old, limiting self-concept with a new and improved one. It's not thinking you're a cowardly storekeeper or a poor teaman, but it's not thinking you're a warrior either. It's not holding any self-concept in mind, but just striking down.

After everyone in the training group has played the part of a salesperson making a presentation to a potential customer, I ask them to list the things that they did well during the role-play and the things they would like to improve upon. Then we discuss the "like-to-improve-upons." Sam says he's no good at thinking on his feet. He goes blank. A real salesman, Sam says, is able to handle himself smoothly.

Gerri says her problem is talking too fast. Her words come shooting out so fast she often says the wrong thing. She gets flustered. She blows sales.

One by one, they all have to tell me about their "improve-upons." Midway through every description of a problem I stop the speaker and say something like "I'm not sure I understand what you mean. I'll tell you what: show me how you would like to be able to do it." Then I just sit back and watch the amazing thing that almost always happens. Virtually every time, they are all able to do what they said they had trouble doing or could not do at all. Sam, for example, actually does think on his feet, and responds smoothly and quickly to the prospect's objections. Gerri actually becomes a more composed, together, non-flustered and relaxed saleswoman. Shy people who wish to act more boldly and self-confidently actually do. Those who wish to improve their body language do so. And tough, defensive people who "always" argue and who want to be more friendly and warm succeed in acting that way.

In the words of the samurai, I have prompted each of the role-players to act directly without letting their self-concept affect their performance at all. They're *doing* before their self-concepts have time to inform them, "You just got through saying you couldn't do that, so it doesn't make any sense for this guy to ask you to."

What the role-players learn is precisely what the sword master taught the teaman: You can do what even you believed you couldn't if you forget about your self-concept totally and just strike.

Mushin and Ushin

"Accept whatever you're doing and flow with whatever may happen."

Chuang Tzu

The perfect action, says Takuan, is one that leaves not a hairbreadth's interval between the urge to action and the action itself. "When a flint strikes steel, a spark immediately issues forth." Samurai Tesshu Yamaoka says, "Cast aside all specific designs and rush to the attack the moment you see your enemy in the act of unsheathing his sword."

The samurai alternative is not concerning yourself with your *self* at all. It is letting no inner view of yourself intervene between the idea of an action and your performance of it. It is sparking immediately, like a flint striking steel. And it is rushing to the attack without concerning yourself with specific opinions about your capabilities.

When you allow nothing to interpose itself between the impulse to action and the action itself—no thoughts such as "I'm not a good extemporaneous speaker and I've got this damned talk to make"—you enter the powerful psychological state of *mushin*. It was the mind state that the sword master coached the poor teaman into. It was the state the samurai always tried to reach when going into battle.

Mushin means "no-mindedness," or "without thought." It doesn't mean living and conducting business without thinking about what you're doing. That's not *mushin*, it's stupidity. *Mushin* means doing whatever you're doing without any thought about your "I ams," "I can'ts" and "I'm nots," or any concern about "what bad thing will happen if I lose this battle" or "what great thing will happen if I win it."

The opposite of *mushin* is *ushin*, "the mind conscious of itself," or *self-consciousness*. You're experiencing *ushin* whenever your internal opinion of yourself makes you concerned with your *self* instead of the action at hand.

When you're in *ushin*, your thoughts about yourself and how you're coming across inhibit you. You worry too much about the importance of winning and the possibility of losing, about what others will think of you and about protecting your own inner view of yourself: "Oh, I could never do that; I'm not good at that kind of thing. It would be embarrassing if I tried and failed."

Here's an *ushin* experience that someone in business is going through right now.

A company vice-president asks you to give a speech "sometime" to about ten executives on new approaches to improving productivity. It's a little scary, but you think, "Listen, it's a chance to get noticed." You say, "Sure."

Two weeks later you receive a memo from the company president stating he will personally attend "this important event." You start thinking, "This is a bigger deal than I thought. Maybe I shouldn't have agreed to do it. But on the other hand if I impress old R.J. I'm on my way."

You read some books and journal articles, only to discover that there's a lot on productivity but just about nothing on "new approaches." You start getting nervous about having anything worthwhile to say.

A few days later you bump into Harry on your way back from the coffee machine. He tells you your speech has been moved up to next Wednesday, and another forty plant managers are flying in for it. You look down and notice your hand shaking and your coffee spilling on Harry's pants.

Tuesday night comes and you're at home nervously trying to organize your speech. You tell yourself, "It just doesn't fit together. It doesn't make sense." You picture yourself at the podium going blank and turning beet-red with embarrassment.

Your little daughter comes in carrying a teddy bear. She asks for a good-night kiss and you're so worried about the speech you kiss the bear by mistake.

Attaching and Non-Attaching

"Victory goes to the one who has no thought of himself."
Shinkage School of Swordsmanship

More than two thousand years ago Chuang Tzu wrote a description of a situation so relevant to contemporary business and personal life that he could have written it yesterday.

He wrote that when an archer is shooting and no external prize is at stake he possesses all his skill. The moment a prize is riding on the shot, even a brass buckle, the archer becomes nervous. If the prize is more valuable, as a quantity of gold, "he shoots as if he were blind."

The archer's skill has not changed, Chuang Tzu says, but the importance the bowman has attached to the prize has made him care too much. Because he is thinking more about winning the prize than simply shooting the arrow, his performance suffers.

Describe this situation to competitive archers of today and you will receive the same response I always do: "Chuang Tzu is exactly right. I shoot much better when I pay no attention to the prize."

You can easily demonstrate the same principle for yourself. Try finding a job when you need one desperately, or making a sale when you *have* to make it or be fired, or asking for a date when you've struck out fourteen consecutive times, or negotiating a contract the loss of which will mean bankruptcy court. When you need to perform *or else,* it's more difficult to win and far easier to lose.

Now think of a time when you didn't desperately need to perform well. It was when you already had a great job that the job offers came. It is always easier to make a sale when you've already surpassed your quota, or to get a date when you're going to have to bump someone else to make room for this one. When the pressure is off, success is easier.

It was the same thing with samurai. From the *kyudo* tradition comes the story of the archer who could shoot with complete calm at ground level, but who broke down when he had to shoot standing at the edge of a cliff.

If you have ever performed better when you didn't need the prize, you have experienced one of the key concepts of samurai fighting—*non-attachment*, the path to *mushin*. It is shooting for the prize, but doing it as if you weren't, and possessing all your skill.

Non-attaching is doing whatever needs to be done, but with the element of self removed. It is being completely engrossed in the action you're engaged in and *nothing else*—not your worries about what might happen, not your visions of your own skill or greatness, not your self-concepting "I ams," "I can'ts" or "I'm nots," not the raise you'll probably get if you win this battle or the date or the sale. Non-attachment is living with all your power directed at one thing and one thing only—whatever is to be accomplished, without any *misai no ichinen*, "trace of thought," left over for anything else.

It is *not* not caring. Non-attachment doesn't mean indifference or lack of concern with what you're doing. It means just the opposite—be vitally concerned with the task in front of you. *But only it.*

Non-attachment is not worrying so much about prizes, results or by-products of your efforts. What the teaman wanted as a by-product of the fight was to live. And he did live, because the sword master taught him not to worry about living or dying or anything else, but only to strike.

When you take the non-attaching approach, you tell yourself: "If prizes of money, fame, praise and honors come my way because of my achievements that's fine, that's wonderful. If my company expands its business, that's great. But when I'm in action I'll do far better once I shelve my thoughts of prizes for a while and just strike, concerning myself only with doing what there is to be done."

Mushin and non-attachment sound "Eastern" but in fact are just as close to Western traditions. In 1899, American psychologist William James observed that people were really trying *too* hard to achieve their goals. He believed that there was a healthier way to operate, one that was far more likely to help people reach their goals. His recommendation was to cut off "egoistic preoccupations" about results. Do that, he said, and ironically the results will be twice as good. What James was saying was: if you wish to double your effectiveness, *non-attach*.

Frederick Herzberg is one of the leading authorities on worker motivation. His extensive research studies found that high satisfaction at work is brought about by factors which he called "satisfiers," and that satisfiers motivated people to superior effort and performance: when satisfiers are in effect, you feel better and you perform better too.

What are the satisfier-motivators? They are factors *intrinsic* to the job, particularly the work itself. Workers are motivated when barriers between themselves and their work are reduced, when they are allowed to focus on the work, can assume *more*—not less—responsibility for it, have more freedom to do the job and are allowed to face new and more difficult tasks.

In their studies of the highest-producing salesmen in all fields, Robert A. Whitney, Thomas Hubin and John D. Murphy found what studies of high producers in any field of business normally find. Although these salesmen usually had higher incomes than the poorer performers, it wasn't attachment to the reward that drove them to work hard: "The doing of a job itself—and doing it successfully—seemed to actually be the thing that motivated them most and brought them greatest satisfaction."* Like the master archer, they thought more of the shooting than of the winning, and because of that they won.

What Herzberg, as well as Whitney, Hubin and Murphy, found to be true of modern business, the samurai knew hundreds of years ago: people will be far more successful in their work when they are able to clear their mind of everything extrinsic to the battle at hand, including self-concepts or rewards, and are able to attend solely to the battle—when they are able to non-attach.

Attaching Management; Non-Attaching Management

Self-concepts, *mushin* (without thought) and *ushin* (self-consciousness) and attachment and non-attachment are bottom-line issues affecting the productivity of entire corporate work forces.

* Robert A. Whitney et al., *The New Psychology of Persuasion and Motivation in Selling* (Englewood Cliffs, N.J.: Prentice-Hall, Inc., 1965), p. 35.

Remember Bill, the fellow who ran the day-to-day operations of an organization of three thousand people? He told me that he wasn't going to make any decisions; he had made that "mistake" the year before. There is more to Bill's story. The reason he didn't intend to make decisions was that he'd made some the previous year that almost got him fired. Bill managed to talk his way out of trouble, but as a result of the experience he was left with a deep scar, a wound from the organizational wars, and it made him afraid to go into battle again. He became a conscientious objector to making decisions.

As Bill confided in me about his fear of making decisions I was reminded of a psychiatrist who once told me that for every "crazy" person in a mental institution there is a person on the outside who drove him crazy, and the one walking around on the outside is the *really* crazy one.

Bill is a product of *attaching management*. It's self-consciousness, *ushin*-creating business leadership. It's crazy-making management that destroys the best aspects of the company's work force by making personnel afraid of making mistakes, fearful of expressing themselves, reluctant to try the new and innovative, secretive and guarded, suspicious of others and defensive. Attaching management makes workers protect themselves against any possible assault from the outside. People and organizations alike have only so much energy. When the energy is directed at protecting the self against attack, it isn't being directed at goals and objectives.

Non-attaching management is very different. Workers in these firms have self-concepts, but they are not constantly under the threat of attack. There is a given in these firms, and it is simply: trust. Trusting management evaluates the quality of a person's performance but not the quality of the person. That the worker is O.K. is a given in non-attachment companies.

Trust goes hand in hand with productivity. Management that is able to rid workers of constant *ushin* self-consciousness, that helps them non-attach instead of attach, increases productivity and personal effectiveness. It enables its work force to be in the most highly productive state of working, to be in *mushin*. On their own, workers will tackle more difficult goals when job-oriented non-attaching management is in effect. Will they under self-oriented attaching management? You know the answer as well as I. No way.

"Your army will win," says Sonshi, "if it is animated by the same high spirit throughout its ranks." To animate it, take its thoughts off itself and let it think only of goals and tasks, let it think only of striking.

Research has shown that non-attaching leads to success in the classroom. If the teacher is able to maintain a non-threatening atmosphere, student productivity—learning—increases. On the other hand, the student who is made to worry excessively about his performance—who attaches—may well develop "performance anxiety." The performance-anxious student doesn't perform as well, usually receives poorer grades and drops out of school more often than the less anxious student of equal intelligence.

All business managers (and all classroom teachers) get the level of output they deserve. If there is something wrong with productivity, look first to someone's failure to create a non-attached environment.

Strategies for Reaching the Samurai Alternative

"Tomorrow's battle is won during today's practice."
Samurai maxim

• Call your self-concept on what it's trying to do. Let it know you see what it's up to. Let's say . . .

—you're about to take a job interview and you're scared silly;

—you see an attractive person, want to ask him/her out but don't because of your shyness dragon;

—you turn down a strategically important opportunity to speak publicly, telling yourself, "I'm a terrible speaker;"

—you worry constantly about the future;

—you dream of making a significant change in your career or private life, but are stopped short of the actual doing when you remind yourself you're not a risk-taker.

  . . . First, alert yourself to the fact that you're out of *mushin* and in *ushin* self-consciousness, and that it's your self-concept that's putting you into it. Then say to yourself, or just think it if you're with other people, "Hey, self-concept, I know you're trying to make me feel . . . (scared, shy, worried, upset). I know you want me to be *ushin* self-conscious. I've

fallen for that in the past, but not now—I'm just going to switch you off
and go ahead without you."

• Fall seven times and get up eight.

Ushin self-consciousness is at work whenever you feel low-spirited
about *having failed* or the *prospect of failing.* The need not to fail in any
enterprise is a power-drainer *extraordinaire.* Give in to that need and the
result will always be the same—*you will settle for less.*

Instead of settling for less in business or life, why not accept failure as
an inevitable part of living? Do that and you will no doubt find what the
following story from the Way of the samurai illustrates—to fail isn't
nearly as harmful as the need not to.

Ten men were forced to escape from their hometown. They had
double trouble: one, to escape safely they would have to climb over a
treacherous mountain, and two, they were all totally blind. Yet they
started out, hand in hand, up the steep mountain trail.

They reached a cliff and all became terror-stricken and unsure of
themselves. Suddenly the lead man fell off. The remaining nine wailed,
"Oh, how awful. How terrible."

Then from below came the cheerful voice of the fallen man. "Don't
be afraid. I'm all right. I landed on a ledge. All the time we were walking
I kept thinking how horrendous it would be if I fell. But I fell and it was
really nothing. If the rest of you want to feel better I suggest you fall as
quickly as you can."

That's the samurai spirit of "Falling seven times and getting up
eight." It applies not only to samurai warfare but to the everyday events
you encounter in business and personal life. If you fall . . . when you
fall . . . just remind yourself to fall seven times and get up eight.

• Pay more attention to the job to be done than to the opinion of
others. One of the major prizes we're shooting for constantly is the
favorable opinion of other people. Most *self*-consciousness is really *other*-
consciousness. Struggle too hard to please others and you'll find yourself
shooting poorly much of the time—even at work.

Whatever you do for a living, there are whole armies of others doing
the same thing. Most of them are indistinguishable from each other
because they are all trying to be what they think they are supposed to be.
Locate the high-excellers and invariably what you'll find is the unique
one who has found what the samurai calls his "original face." He's pay-
ing attention to what he wants, not what others tell him he should want.

• Be ready for others to try to make you re-attach yourself to them. Your self-concept is not your private property; it's under joint ownership. When you start stepping out of your self-concept and acting differently, invariably somebody is going to tell you to return to your unit.

The landmark Hawthorne studies of worker productivity revealed that work groups' norms can restrict output. When a "new guy" was found to be working too hard he was told by old-timers to slow down. If he didn't, he was told again. If he persisted he was "binged"—hit sharply and powerfully on the shoulder till he got the message.

From day one of your life there have been people around to tell you you're a good person or a louse, a competent worker or a bungler, one of God's chosen or one of the damned, a good student or a poor one, outgoing or introverted, smart or dumb, a sweetheart or a sourpuss. Parents, teachers, friends, co-workers and others are constantly telling you what kind of person you are and "should" be. They're binging you back into their concept of you all the time. Be ready for it to happen, because it will.

• Try being less careful and more spontaneous. Practice throwing caution to the wind every once in a while. Don't give yourself the time to wrap yourself up in *ushin* self-consciousness. Just strike like lightning.

• Think more of shooting than winning. Remember the paradox of non-attachment: shoot for nothing and you have all your skill, but shoot for a prize of gold and you'll be drained of power. Stop thinking of all that's riding on your action, from "Will she go out with me?" to "Will I make the sale?" Just ask her out; just sell.

• Refuse to blame yourself. Self-blame—for shortcomings, failures, falls and defeats—will rocket you right out of *mushin* and into self-consciousness. Instead of blaming, try forgiving yourself.

• Value effort, not just success. An attitude of "Winning isn't everything, it's the *only* thing," simply won't wash in most business or personal situations. Constantly worrying about being perfect is *ushin.* The only thing that's perfect is your perfect right to make mistakes.

• Evaluate your performance, not yourself. If everyone at the table leaves your stew uneaten, you might want to take a look at your culinary abilities. When your sales performance starts skidding, if you're wise you will take a good, hard look at the causes, which may in fact be in you. But—and it's an important but—adamantly refuse to tie your self-respect to *any* performance. Never confuse what you do with what you're worth. That's attaching. Rate your performance, but don't rate yourself.

You can begin by always asking yourself *performance-oriented* rather than *personality-oriented* questions. Instead of "Am I any good at making money?" ask yourself, "How can I make money?" Rather than "Do I really belong in sales?" ask yourself, "How can I learn to sell more effectively?"

Final Words on Reaching the Samurai Alternative

• Your self-concept is your inner belief about the kind of person you are and what you are and are not capable of.

• Countless people are losing their battles not because they lack ability, but because they are confined by a narrow self-concept.

• The *storekeeper option* is replacing a limiting self-concept with a more useful one.

• The *samurai alternative* is operating without a self-estimate, but with *mushin,* "no-mindedness." It's casting aside all specific designs, even designs about who you are, and rushing to the attack.

• *Ushin* is "the mind conscious of itself," or self-consciousness. An *ushin* mind is an uptight one.

• Archers who think too much about winning prizes don't shoot very well. Whatever you're shooting for, you're more likely to hit it if you've non-attached, shifting your attention from the winning to the act of shooting.

7

Slaying Your Emotional Dragons

"Fast as the wind; quiet as the forest; aggressive as fire; and immovable as a mountain."

Samurai Shingen Takeda's battle banner

The Battle on the Uji River

"A samurai lives and dies with his sword in hand."

Kiyomasa Kato, sixteenth-century
samurai general

On a June day in 1180, fifty samurai of the Minamoto clan under the command of Yorimasa were holed up south of Kyoto in the villa of Byodo-in on the Uji River. Among them were many of the finest warriors in all Japan. With them were two hundred and fifty *sohei*, well-trained warrior monks.

At dawn, after dressing for battle and cleaning their weapons, the three hundred soldiers walked to the huge gate and waited for it to be opened. As soon as it was, the three hundred raced out and attacked the waiting enemy who could be seen dimly through the fog on the River—twenty thousand troops of the Taira clan!

The bridge was narrow; and so, to be the first to reach the Taira, some of the Minamoto samurai climbed over the backs of the men in front of them.

All fifty of the Minamoto and the *sohei* with them were killed in this action. But their spirit of bravery united the great Minamoto warriors who, when they heard news of their fifty clan-brothers, left their homes to take up arms against the powerful Taira family.

The war raged for five years. When it was over, the Minamoto were rulers of all Japan and hardly one Taira warrior who had fought that day at Uji remained alive.

We think of those three hundred and say, "Imagine attacking twenty thousand men! Those guys were fearless."

Are we right? *There is no way of telling.*

Some of the three hundred had perhaps reached the samurai ideal of *fudoshin*, "immovable mind." It is a mind totally committed to facing any fate or circumstance life throws at you with calm composure. It's being able to endure pain and hardship with indifference.

Sword master Ichiun Odagiri said that even in a fight to the death the *fudoshin* samurai has the appearance of a man to whom nothing special is happening. To others he looks like someone who is doing nothing more dangerous than "sitting at the breakfast table."

A prisoner being tortured by his captors said, "If you keep bending my arm back like that you'll break it."

There was a loud snap as bone broke. The prisoner said, "See? I was right." That's *fudoshin*.

Samurai Musashi altered the term *fudoshin* to *iwao no mi*, "rock body." He was asked to define "rock body." As is the Japanese way, instead of explaining he demonstrated. He commanded one of his students to commit *seppuku*, suicide by disembowelment, also called *hara-kiri*, "belly cutting." As the student was about to plunge the dagger into his stomach and begin the horribly painful pulling-across-then-upward cut, Musashi stopped him. "That's rock body," he said.

While probably some of the three hundred Minamoto had immovable minds and rock bodies, it is quite possible that some of them didn't. It is very possible that as they stood waiting for the gate to be opened some were coming face to face with inner opponents, the same dragons that we encounter in our business and personal lives—worry, anxiety, depression, feelings of inferiority, self-doubt, nervousness and others.

Could it be that some of the three hundred were even afraid? Certainly! It is even possible that every single one of them was absolutely terrified.

The samurai was aware that 70 percent of his battles were with inner dragons, and that fear was at the heart of them. He peered right into the eyes of his opponents, even this one, and concluded: "Fear is the true enemy, the only enemy." He would have come to precisely the same conclusion if he were alive today.

Fear is as much a part of business as a briefcase or a pen, and as much a part of living as breathing. From fear of making a decision or of taking a chance, to the fear of going to the dentist's, of flying or dying, of tomorrow, of fear itself, and on and on—a catalogue of business and personal fears.

For all that we don't know what the three hundred Minamoto were experiencing *inside,* there is something we do know. It is the essence of the samurai Way, the core element of effective action in business and personal life.

Whatever the three hundred were experiencing internally, to a man they advanced.

The "fudoshins" advanced. No surprise there. Leaping into battle was easy for them. It felt no different than eating breakfast.

But even those who were afraid advanced. Self-doubters advanced, and the timid along with them. Those who felt like retreating for *any* reason went forward anyway. Every one of them raced forward *zan-totsu,* closing and striking.

Attention

"The end of our Way of the sword is to be fearless when confronting our inner enemies and our outer enemies."
Tesshu Yamaoka, nineteenth-century *kendo* master

A layman asked a Zen master to write some words containing the greatest wisdom.

The master picked up his brush and wrote, "Attention."

"I was hoping for something more," the disappointed layman said.

"More?" the master asked, picking up his brush and writing again—this time, "Attention. Attention."

"That's it?" asked the layman.

The master had been expecting that. This time he wrote it three times: "Attention, Attention, Attention."

Your ability to choose how you will direct your attention is your most powerful weapon. That is an overriding theme of this book. The warrior's most vital skill is what judo master Kan'emon Terada called *karada o shite seishin ni jujun narashimeru jutsu*, "the skill of making the body obey the mind."

It's where your mind is focused that determines the outcome of your battles—with a business competitor, with a heaping dish of ice cream that's out to destroy your diet, or with laziness or fear or any other inner opponent. The samurai guide *Hagakure* says: "There is only the one purpose of the present moment. A person's whole life is a succession of present moments." It is exactly what those Minamoto troops knew, and every samurai along with them—the Way of the samurai is intentional moment-to-moment choice. It is directing your attention in such a way that you consciously choose the thoughts, emotions and actions that will lead to victory over anything standing between you and where you want to be—and making those choices from moment to moment and time and time again.

Cutting Off Your Thoughts

"Success will always be yours when your heart is without disturbance."

Itto school of swordsmanship,
sixteenth century

Bukko's Advice to Tokimune Hojo

Tokimune was only eighteen years old when his father died and he became shogunal regent of Japan. He was very intelligent, but he suffered from fears and worries. Under normal circumstances he might have been able to rule well in spite of them. But even as he was assuming the throne the greatest event in Japanese history was beginning, the great Mongolian invasions of Japan.

Tokimune had the good sense to realize that if he personally was cowardly Japan would probably be overrun by the enemy, led by the great Kubilai Khan.* The only chance for victory depended on Tokimune's being the courageous rock body, the immovable mind from which his samurai would draw their confidence and the will to win. Deeply troubled, the young regent called on the Zen master Bukko for help.

Tokimune said, "Of all the enemies in life, the worst is fear. How can I be liberated from it?"

Bukko replied, "You must cut it off at the place it comes from."

"And where," asked Tokimune, "does fear come from?"

"It comes from Tokimune," Bukko answered.

"I hate fear above everything else. How can you say it comes from me?"

"Try and see how you feel about it when you abandon the self you call Tokimune. I'll see you when you've done that."

"How do I abandon Tokimune?"

"Simply cut off your thoughts."

The regent left to try out this advice.

Some time afterward Tokimune received news that the Mongol armada carrying forty thousand troops had set sail for Japan. The fight was on! Dressed in his armor, the young regent went to visit Bukko before the battle. "The great moment has come," Tokimune said.

"Is there any way you can avoid it?" Bukko asked, playing devil's advocate.

Without hesitation Tokimune gave a loud battle cry. He was ready!

Though Tokimune died of natural causes at the young age of thirty-three, he lived to see the Mongols vanquished, a defeat owed in great part to the courage of a man who had to acquire it to save his country.

There are two main methods for overcoming the emotional dragons you encounter day to day, in business and personal life. Both are based on Bukko's advice to "simply cut off your thoughts." In Thought-Cut-

* The name "Kubilai Khan" is Koppitsuretsu in Japanese.

ting Method One, you replace one thought with another; in Thought-Cutting Method Two, you eliminate your dragons through action.

Thought-Cutting Method One: Thought-Replacement

Our emotions don't simply happen to us willy-nilly, but are caused by our thoughts. The insight that we choose our emotions, including our dragons, as surely as we select items off a menu has long been a part of Eastern ways. "All we are is the result of what we have thought," says the *Dhammapada* of Buddhism. Master Torajiro Okada said, "The meaning of all things is within, in your mind, not something that exists 'out there.'" The *shin-ki-ryoku* formula of chapter four—your thoughts make energy make power—also points to the impact of a person's thoughts on his emotions. That thoughts, not events, determine your emotions is an understanding now firmly entrenched in Western psychology: you feel how you think. Succinctly, here is how you create your emotions:

1. You encounter an event.
2. You make evaluations about the event.
3. You feel an emotion that is caused by your evaluations.

Your emotion is never "in" the event; it is always in how you evaluate it.

It might seem that your boss makes you furious when he dresses you down, but in fact it is your thoughts that cause your emotion, not your boss. Emotions are always added ingredients, even in crisis situations. Late one night a samurai general asleep in his home was awakened by one of his men.

"We must run for it," the soldier said. "The house is on fire."

The general rubbed his eyes. "Where is the fire now?"

"It is in the kitchen, but it's spreading fast."

"In the kitchen, you say. See to it that you wake me again when it reaches the hallway beyond my door."

He put his head down and fell back asleep.

Getting laid off certainly seems to be a natural depression generator, but in reality this emotional dragon, like all the others, is your own creation. Just think how differently you would feel if you had another job already lined up and you wanted to get laid off so you could collect severance pay. Same objective event—you're handed a pink slip—but very different evaluations of the event. Instead of "Oh hell, this is awful," you're thinking "Hallelujah!" and feeling wonderful.

At times the leap from event to emotion is so fast that it seems there is no evaluation stage at all. But if you could use instant replay to capture the leap and play it back in slow motion, mental sound track and all, you would find your thoughts assessing the event.

Excessive anger is often the result of lightning-fast thought habits, and it's one of the fighter's main bugaboos. The samurai maxim "An angry man will defeat himself in battle and life too" is just as true today. Just look at the figures on high blood pressure and other stress-related diseases. Every day angry people are defeating themselves. They're making their bodies obey their mind all right, and it's killing them.

To see for yourself that it's you who's in charge of your feelings, practice going back and forth from negative to positive emotions. When you're feeling down, think over to the positive, then back to the negative, then to the positive again. You'll see how really easy it is to control your feelings any time you wish to. All you have to do is choose your thoughts.

Once we know that we think ourselves into emotions, it's a short step to: *a way to overcome any emotional dragon standing in your way is to evaluate events differently.*

"Simply cut off your thoughts," as Bukko said, and think differently. You don't alter the facts of the situation, but you do consciously, purposely and intentionally change the meaning you attach to the facts. If there are twenty thousand Taira waiting for you outside, or three important sales prospects across the table, those are the unalterable facts. The facts may be unalterable but your thoughts are very alterable. You can choose to think what you will—confidence-producing thoughts or "Oh my Lord" fear-producers. You can choose to think any thought you want whenever you want.

All of a warrior's skills are based on the development of habits that will serve him well. Here the habit you must develop is to direct your attention, time and time again, to thinking the thoughts that will create the emotions you want, and defeat your emotional dragons in the process.

If you would normally think, "I'm not going to get the job anyway, so why should I bother with this interview," you now eliminate that thought and evaluate the situation differently. "I've got as good a shot as anybody else."

For every "I'm depressed because my hair is turning grey" or "What hair? I'm going bald," try a more realistic evaluation: "The color of my hair or even my having just one live follicle on my head has absolutely nothing to do with who I really am."

If you're a salesman and you stumble while walking into a prospect's office, try replacing "I'm a clumsy oaf" thoughts with "That's a lie. I'm not clumsy, but I am human, and like anyone else might do, I just stumbled. Big deal."

Instead of "I'm a failure because I didn't get the report done on time," tell yourself that what you're really saying is "I'm sorry I didn't get it done on time. But in no way does that make me a failure."

Instead of "Oh damn, am I worried," think, "Worry helps nothing and nobody. Only action helps."

Tokimune's main dragon was fear. It might be yours, but it might not be. Whatever yours is, look it right in the eye. Be able to say, "I'm constantly blowing my stack. I realize that." Or, "I'm depressed a lot of the time." Or, "I'm a worrywart. Other people live with gusto. I live with tension."

Remind yourself that whatever the dragon is, you're creating it by directing your attention in a way that is harming you. Direct it consciously and intentionally to thinking the thoughts that will produce the opposite emotion.

Thought-Cutting Method Two: Destroying Dragons Through Action

> "The Way of the sword is like crossing a stream on a log bridge. It takes concentrating and moving."
>
> Kendo tradition

A sage watched snow falling on a small branch of a willow tree. As the snow accumulated, the branch bent flexibly under the load and the snow slid off. Other branches that didn't bend snapped from the weight of the snow.

A river adapts to a rock in its way by flowing around it. In this way the river eventually erodes the rock.

One day two thousand years ago Chang San-Feng, the creator of tai chi, watched a crane fighting a snake. The crane was much larger and more powerful and had a swordlike beak and sharp talons. But no matter how hard it stabbed or struck it couldn't hit the snake. Twisting and writhing, the snake was always out of reach. When the crane was exhausted the snake coiled once and lashed out, killing it with one venomous bite.

Each of these vignettes illustrates an important element of the warrior's Way and of Oriental life generally. *Ju* means flexibility, pliancy, suppleness and adaptability. Judo (ju-do) literally means the Way of defeating your opponent by adapting to his moves and personality. It doesn't matter if it's an outer opponent or an inner dragon you're fighting, or if the fighter is a person or a business firm, *the warrior wins by adapting to changing circumstances.*

All living things, whether they're people, plants or businesses, *are* living because they're able to adapt.

As you read about Japanese management look for the word "flexibility." You might be surprised to see how often it's used. *Ju*, flexible adaptation, affects every aspect of the successful business firm, from how it markets, advertises and sells its products to how it designs its organization and how it leads and motivates its personnel. The firm that's alive and growing is the one which adapts to changing conditions, like the snake or the river or the small willow branch.

The skilled bowman quickly adapts *(ju)* his position and aim as his target moves. Substitute "business" for "bowman" and "consumer" for "target" in the preceding sentence and you have a description of effective business operation. The successful corporation (and government agency and educational institution) adapts as fast as a warrior to the changing needs and desires of consumers. The company may discontinue a line, modify a product or develop a totally new one—*whatever* it takes to satisfy the ever-moving consumer.

The unsuccessful organization is the one which finds it hard to adapt adequately or quickly enough to conditions in the marketplace. For bowmen and manufacturers alike, the consequences of an inability to adapt are precisely the same—they lose.

The field of advertising is an art of *ju*, flexible adaptability. Successful advertising prompts a consumer to take notice, absorb information and, most important, to act—to buy the product or use the service. The *only* advertising that will succeed is that which is adapted to the consumer's psychology—the interests, drives and motivations of the target audience. The more precise the *ju* adaptation, the more powerful the advertising— bull's-eye.

Ju, or flexible adaptability, also affects the design of the company. Extensive research backs up the claim that there is no single best organizational model or pattern. The structure necessary to succeed in one industry may be as different from the design that will bring success in another field as granite is from putty. But what is always necessary if the firm is to succeed is the ability to adapt to the conditions in which that particular firm operates.

Motivation, that magical word, is one of the major keys to a person's and a company's economic well-being. Put a turtle with motivation and a hare with only speed on the starting blocks, then get the blue ribbon ready for the turtle.

In the past, business managers believed that the one best way to motivate the worker was through financial rewards—money. More recently it has been found that money is just one of a wide variety of motivators, and that motivational incentives vary from person to person. What may be a tremendously potent motivator to you and can literally send you charging up the ladder of success may be totally powerless to budge your dearest friend even one inch. Given the enormously wide-ranging differences in workers' motivations, what are business managers to do? The answer, of course, is to apply *ju* and flexibly adapt to the motivators that work for each individual employee.

Corporate managers who are particularly effective are practitioners of *ju,* adaptability. All managers have a preferred style of management, one they're best at using and feel most comfortable with. The most effective manager is the one who maintains his best style but has a second or third that he can slip into when the situation is appropriate. The same is true of all skilled fighters. The best style is the one that works in any particular situation.

We owe our existence—as a species and individually—to *ju,* adaptability. We might be puny compared to the dinosaurs, but we are able to adapt, and they couldn't. It's what the fighter knows: size makes no difference at all; *ju* makes all the difference.

The human body is a *ju*-based system. When it's invaded by germs it adapts by creating antibodies whose job is to annihilate the invader.

The ultimate in *ju* is inner, mental *ju*. It is being able to respond to all circumstances life throws at you without your attention being blocked by any emotion. It's letting no fear or any other dragon prevent you from doing what the action requires. The Minamoto at the Uji River had inner *ju*. Samurai in general had it, and many successful people in all areas of business and private life have it.

Millionaire insurance man W. Clement Stone directed his attention into a fortune. During the first years of his sales career, whenever he even approached the entrances of large institutions such as banks, railroad offices and department stores he became "exceedingly frightened" and he passed them by. He had been afraid of selling to smaller institutions too, but had learned to "neutralize" his fears. He then used the same approach with the bigger ones. He discovered that hardly any of the personnel in the large establishments had been contacted at all. Why? Because salesmen in general were afraid of approaching them.

"Speechophobia," the fear of speaking before a group: most Americans rank it higher in their fear hierarchy than dying, which comes in sixth. In other words, for most people, being on that bridge with the Minamoto samurai is chicken feed compared with having to make a speech.

What makes an effective speaker? Is it being speechophobia-free? Not necessarily. Research is revealing that people who are effective public speakers often report experiencing the same type of nervous butterflies as the poor speaker. The difference is that effective speakers go ahead anyway, in spite of what they're feeling. They go into action, taking their butterflies along with them.

Inner *Ju* Insights

Wherever you find inner *ju* people, from standing at a bridge ready to die with sword in hand to raising a family or selling insurance, they invariably share the following warrior's insights:

• There is no such thing as feeling perfectly fit and exactly right for action; there are only actions that are there to be carried out.

If you waited until you felt just right before doing something, from jogging to making your big life-move, there's hardly anything you would do.

• No one is totally and forever dragon-free; there are just people who are stopped by their dragons and others who aren't.

All actions of any importance require daring. Fear of one sort or another is always a partner to business, *budo* (the Way of the samurai) and personal life. Thought-Cutting Method One, thought-replacement, will help defeat many dragons, but to expect to be completely dragon-free all the time is asking too much. There is a wonderful Japanese saying: "Even monkeys fall out of trees," *Ki kara saru mo ochiru.* Monkeys fall, and men and women at times worry, at times fear.

• *Fudoshin,* immovable mind, is accessible to anyone every day.

Have you ever run in a marathon, felt pain, thought of stopping but refused to? If so, you have tasted *fudoshin.* Your mind was immovable. It wouldn't budge from the goal of finishing.

You're lying in bed, feeling like staying in the warm cocoon of blankets instead of braving the traffic, the snow and an unpleasant meeting. But you get up anyway. That's everyday, nuts-and-bolts *fudoshin.* It's the skill of making the body obey the mind.

The *fudoshin* of the samurai was making that kind of choice time and again.

• You can carry your dragons right into battle with you and win anyway.

Neither W. Clement Stone nor the effective public speakers overcame their inner opponents before they moved. They went right into action—fear, trepidation, butterflies and all. They were like the Minamoto at the Uji River who were afraid but went ahead anyway.

Every day in offices, streets and livingrooms the people who are operating differently are legion. Their thinking is: "In order to do it (whatever *it* is) I've got to first overcome my problem—my fear (or shyness, lack of self-confidence, bad habits, indecisiveness, etc.). Once I get rid of that baby, I'll be all right. *Then* I'll be able to sell (or lead company staff, make a speech in the town hall, go on a diet, etc.)."

The real problem isn't what they think it is. It is not the fear. It's their belief that the fear has the power to prevent them from doing the *it.*

• If you forget about yourself and your dragons completely and focus only on adapting to what the battle requires of you, no dragon will ever stop you.

It is very possible to live a worry-less–achieve-more life-style by directing your attention *away* from the emotional dragons and *to* the activity, and doing it time and time and time again.

You can feel terrified of making a sales presentation and make it anyway—and do a very fine job—if you take your attention from the terror and move ahead.

Inside you might be enduring shrinking-violet shyness, but you can direct your attention to going to a party and have a great time.

You might be depressed about something at the office, but you can remove your attention from it—consciously, intentionally—and work very effectively.

You can direct your attention away from any inner opponent and *to* the action any time you want to.

• You are a river; your emotional blocks are rocks. By moving forward you erode them.

One benefit of Thought-Cutting Method Two is that you accomplish more when your dragons can't stop you. A second is that you erode the emotional block. You wear it down over the course of time. It's gradual. It takes time. It's slaying your dragons by what the samurai called "chewing at the corners." It's whittling the dragons down.

Guidelines for Directing Your Attention to Eliminate Emotional Dragons

• Start with the realization that although there are hundreds of factors you cannot control in battle, life or business, you *can* control your attention. Your choice powers are your greatest powers, and none is greater than your ability to choose where you will direct your attention.

• Add this insight from *Hagakure:* "There is only the one purpose of the present moment. A person's whole life is a succession of present moments." It is in the moment, this moment, every moment, that the pattern of your life is being laid out. The choices of attention you make in the moment determine your success or failure against any opponent, inner or outer.

If you find yourself constantly worried, afraid or self-doubting, it's due principally to bad habits of moment-to-moment attention. Thought-Cutting Method One stops your attention from thinking harmful, dragon-producing thoughts and consciously replaces those thoughts with more useful ones.

• Form the habit of directing your attention *to* action and *away* from inner opponents. Samurai *fudoshin*, "immovable mind," and *iwao no mi*, "rock body," sound mysterious but aren't. They are merely products of the moment-to-moment choices of the samurai, day after day, never to run from an opponent but to stand immovable as a rock. When you choose to make your body move even if it doesn't feel like it, you have reached the ultimate in *ju*, adaptability.

You can acquire *fudoshin* and wear down your emotional blocks by consciously choosing to do something *because* it seems a little "scary" or unpleasant. Sounding very much like a samurai, psychologist William James wrote: ". . . be systematically heroic every day in little unnecessary things; do something every other day for the sole and simple reason that it is difficult and you would prefer not to do it, so that when the cruel hour of danger strikes, you will not be unnerved or unprepared."

• Don't use force; just nudge your attention away from the emotional block and to the action. That's very important. The "law of reverse effects" is one to remember. It says that if you think too much about *not* doing something you tend to do it. It's one big reason why people who have been on diets for thirty-five years sometimes weigh more now than they did thirty-six years ago.

Don't dwell on what you *shouldn't* feel—"Damn it, I will overcome this fear." Just ease your attention over to what you want to accomplish, completely forgetting about the dragon. Say, "I can choose to direct my attention any way I want. I'm choosing to right now." Don't force, just nudge.

• Exaggerate your emotions before going into action. Operating this way, you don't attempt to alter your evaluations. Instead you direct your attention at *exaggerating* what you're saying to yourself to create the dragon. Take fear, for example. Set aside "fear time"—a few minutes is all it takes—and think fear-inducing thoughts to your heart's content. Fear with reckless abandon. Say the most fearful things you can to yourself. Really put yourself into it. If your body begins to shake nervously, try to add to it. If you're like most people your fear will simply stop on its own.

• Disconnect yourself from the dragon. Each time you use an "I am" you make what follows a part of you. "I am sad . . . angry . . . insulted, depressed, discouraged," etc. You'll feel totally different when you remove the "I." Rather than "I'm depressed," say, "A depression is trying to catch hold of me." Instead of "I'm shy," say, "There's a shyness here." By breaking the connection you remove the emotion from yourself and put it "out there," where it is far easier to deal with.

• Laugh. When you catch yourself face to face with an emotional dragon, race to higher ground and look down. Say, "There's (your name) being scared stiff." Being able to lighten up and laugh is a wonderful dragon-slayer. Not in a cruel, self-critical way, but in the spirit of "Things seem terrible now, but they're not *that* bad."

• Use a right-now timing. Whether you choose Thought-Cutting Methods One or Two, exaggerating the emotion, disconnecting yourself from it, laughter or any combination of these, use it before the dragon gets the upper hand. Striking your opponent at the outset, as soon as you notice it, is the best timing to use against any emotional dragon.

PART THREE

GI
Technique

3

Technique

8

Making the Power Decision

"To fight and conquer in one hundred battles is not the highest
skill. To subdue the enemy with no fight at all, that's the highest
skill."

Sonshi

The power decision is not only an extremely important one, but one you
have absolutely no choice but to make. You have power—far more than
you probably realize—and you *have* to use it. Whether your opponent is
someone else—an outer opponent—or an inner adversary like your own
bad habits, your fears, or any other inner block to success, you'll have to
use some form of power to deal with it. *How* you use it is up to you—
that's the power decision.

Of Swords and Men

"When you reach real ability you will be able to become one with
the enemy. Entering his heart you will see that he is not your
enemy after all."

Tsuji (1650–1730), sword master

The legend goes that the blades fashioned by the swordsmith Muramasa drew their wearers into bloody battle. If you carried a Muramasa-made sword you were constantly in fights. A test was conducted. A Muramasa sword was placed blade up into a stream to determine how it would affect the leaves floating past it on the surface of the water. Each leaf that touched the sword was sliced cleanly in two. Then a sword produced by Masamune, Muramasa's teacher and the greatest of all Japanese swordsmiths, was placed in the stream. One by one the leaves avoided the blade and floated by untouched.*

Every day, in and out of business, we encounter Muramasas and Masamunes. Muramasas are always ready to fight. Masamunes are able to fight, but keep their swords sheathed until they absolutely need them. As a matter of fact, there's a Muramasa and a Masamune in all of us, each vying for supremacy. The Muramasa inside you tells you that if you're to win battles you've got to outdo, outsmart and outmuscle your competitors. You've got to do unto them before they do unto you. On the other hand, the Masamune in you says that many of the conflicts you experience are caused by your being too ready to fight and not willing enough to cooperate.

Where you find an effective business—in Japan, the U.S. or anywhere else—you will also find a business which internally maintains effective *communication, collaboration* and *cooperation* between units—the three C's. I was called in by an organization whose productivity was very low. My analysis of the situation showed that the low productivity was directly related to the *absence* of the three C's between two big units.

Taking the frontal position, I initiated a number of meetings to bring unit management together to face the problem. Over the years the disagreements between the two units had settled into Muramasa-hard toughness, with each unit literally being out to get the other.

The first part of the first meeting consisted of one Muramasa attack after another—such as "You're messing us up on purpose and we aren't about to let you get away with it."

But the moment I had them stop attacking and turned both sides'

* Muramasa swords were considered particularly unlucky by the Tokugawa clan. Ieyasu's son and grandfather were beheaded by Muramasa blades, and as a child Ieyasu was accidentally cut by one. Masamune swords, on the other hand, brought good luck. As a gift of peace after the bloody war with Ieyasu, Hideyoshi Toyotomi presented him with a fine Masamune short-sword. When a man succeeded to the shogunate he was handed a sword as a symbol of his new office. It was a Masamune.

attention to what they both *really* wanted, the potential for Masamune cooperation became clear. *Both* sides wanted to do a good job and be respected; both wanted the organization to prosper and consumers to be pleased; and both wanted to get rid of the bad feelings they had toward the other unit, to improve their departmental and personal performance and *not* to have to fight each other all the time!

Together, as one body, the units decided on specific steps they would take to change from Muramasas to Masamunes. One was this: whenever the Muramasa desire surfaced in a person—i.e., the desire to fight with or sabotage the efforts of the other unit—that person was to arrange a meeting to calmly talk things over with the prospective object of the attack.

There are various laws of expectation, all of which point out that most of the time the life we live is a creation of what we expect. Findings of the behavioral sciences show that, if you expect another person to be cooperative and you act accordingly, you will be proven correct in almost every instance, even if that person has a reputation for being hard to get along with. If you expect the opposite and act accordingly, you will find noncooperation in almost every instance. Muramasas constantly expect fights and, not surprisingly, find them much of the time. Masamunes expect cooperation and receive it most of the time.

The samurai point of view is that it's always best to avoid a fight if you can help it. The *ken no shinzui*, or "real goal," of swordsmanship is to win your battles without "pulling out your sword," *nukazu ni sumu*. Expect cooperation and goodwill and you'll get it most of the time. Remember the samurai attitude, "The greatest victory is the fight not fought." If you're more of a Masamune that shouldn't be too hard for you. But if you're a hardcore Muramasa you'll probably have to work at it.

Drawing your weapon is a serious business. It's not to be taken lightly. It was so grave an act to the samurai that to return his sword to the scabbard without using it was considered an insult to the weapon and the wearer. Drawing your sword is something you'll want to think twice about. Ieyasu Tokugawa wrote, "The right use of the sword is that it should subdue the enemy while lying gleaming in its scabbard."

While the height of fighting skill is to win without fighting at all, there are times when you must draw your sword, and having drawn it must use it with all the power you can. There are two ways to use your power. You can use either one when you make your power decision. One is the direct force-against-force approach. Here you use your power against your opponent's. The second is indirect. It's putting the opponent's power to your use.

Using Force Against Force

Some of the martial arts, like karate and *tae kwon do*, use a direct force-against-force approach to fighting. Their emphasis is on *chikara*, the strength of physical exertion and power. The *karateka* uses his muscles to drive directly through his target. Strength is the key, and so practitioners often lift weights to build it up.

We Americans place a high value on directness, on "shooting from the hip," on "looking a person straight in the eye" and on "getting to the point." And that is exactly how we normally use our power—in a straight, forceful line, to the point of our objective and through our opponents (or problems or disagreements), in exactly the way a *karateka* kicks through a wooden board. In and out of business we're a nation that values *chikara*, muscle power. We're taught to use whatever power we can muster against our opponents, and if they want to fight back they oppose their power to ours. You can see this my-power-against-your-power approach in operation all the way from schoolyards to corporate boardrooms. You shove me; then I shove you. We grapple for a while until one subdues the other. Usually the stronger fighter wins the battle, and so if you're a little guy against a powerful bigger guy you've got a problem.

But there's an irony here. While we often choose to use our force against others, we don't like it when they use theirs against us. And on top of that, while direct power approaches *appear* to work, they're probably not as effective as you might think. Direct *chikara* power approaches are almost totally outmoded in dealing with other people when mutual gain is the objective.

Think of your own opinion of aggressive, "pushy" salespersons. They are probably among the most unpopular figures in all of business because of the way they try to use their power. Nor do we like to see others pushed around. We sympathize with the underdogs—the early New

York Mets, the little guy who single-handedly stands against powerful machine politics, the American ice hockey team that beat the great Russian squad in the 1980 Olympics. At one point the American public was sympathetic to the complaints of Iran against the exiled Shah. But the moment the Khomeini government used overt force, seizing our embassy personnel in Tehran and holding them hostage, the tide of American sentiment turned against Iran with a vengeance. To use force in this way was a total strategic misreading of the psychology of Americans.

American workers dislike being forced by management. If they feel their boss is making them do something, they will resist if they can. Some of the classical studies in management were conducted at the Western Electric plant in a suburb of Chicago. In one of the studies, six young women making telephone assemblies were observed over a long period of time. The object was to determine the effects on output of frequency and length of breaks, the length of the work day, working conditions and other factors. The women were asked to participate in a study, were separated from the rest of the work force, assigned to a less bossy supervisor they considered particularly good and given greater control over how they carried out the work. For example, they could speed up or slow down the conveyor belt whenever they wished.

It was found that no matter what was done to the working conditions, production increased. It continued to rise when the women worked without breaks; longer, more fatiguing days; and even when the lighting in the work area was reduced to the level of moonlight!

There had been complaints before the study that the conveyor belt moved too fast and that it was exhausting trying to keep up. Yet when the women could regulate the speed as they wished—when control was in their hands—they actually made it go faster. Productivity improved and morale along with it.

A key explanation of these results was that the women no longer felt they were being forced to do things by company management, but were making voluntary choices. The real issue with the conveyor, for example, was not its speed, but who had the power to regulate that speed.

Participative management, quality circles, management by objectives and flex-time have each achieved some popularity in American business. And each is based on the simple idea that the best way to get workers to contribute more fully to their work is to actively involve them in making decisions affecting their job. If you *force* them they will probably fight, but if you *involve* them they are likely to contribute.

The autocratic business manager who is highly directive with his subordinates, who plows through their need for choices, sense of professionalism and desire to stamp their work with their own individual style is exactly like the karate expert who uses similar straight-line power to smash through bricks. While there is some pleasure in using power in this way—if it's you using it—it's no fun if you're the brick, and once the brick is destroyed you can't use it to build anything. One of the chief problems in American business life and in our everyday dealings with others is that we have too many people breaking each other's bricks.

Putting Your Opponent's Power to Your Use

"When the opponent comes, welcome him; when he goes, send him on his way." *Kureba mukae, sareba okuru.*

The Way of judo

The karate approach is not the only one. Other fighting systems like aikido, tai chi and judo place little confidence in physical strength and direct power moves. Theirs is the art of using power indirectly.

Many people consider the *indirect approach* in fighting and business to be uniquely Oriental. It's based on avoiding head-on confrontations but exploiting your opponent's power instead—using it to accomplish your ends.

In judo you're taught not to oppose power with power. When your opponent pushes, you don't resist by using a straight-line force to push back; rather, you pull. When your opponent pulls at you, you push. If you meet pushes with pulls and pulls with pushes in your business and personal life, you'll win more often than you ever thought possible. Either way your opponents will be placed in an off-balance position that will render them vulnerable to your counterattack.

Using your power indirectly is based on sensing your attackers' intention and *helping them go in the direction they're headed.* You don't attempt to oppose them, not at all. Instead, you assist them in going the way their power is carrying them. You make use of their power of attack, by directing it to defeat them. You use your opponents' strength and intention. You double your power by using yours *and* theirs. You're doing precisely what Takuan advised: make use of your opponent's attack; "then his sword meant to kill you becomes your own and the weapon will fall on the opponent himself."

Similarly, the essence of aikido is never to oppose an aggressor's power head on, but to redirect it. Aikido is different from judo, however, in that the *aikidoka* continually applies the principle of *marui*, or "circular motion." Rather than meeting an attack head on, you turn and twist. You slide off your opponents. You minimize the impact of the attack and channel it in a direction that you control. As with judo, you place the opponent where his power is leading. Your adversary is led to his own destruction by being "helped" in the direction that his body is already moving.

Using the circular motion of *marui*, it's possible to meet and control an attack of any force from any and all directions. A very skilled *aikidoka* can throw seven, eight, even ten attackers. So confident are practitioners of aikido of this that they call the attacker *uke*, from a Japanese word that suggests falling. Attack a trained *aikidoka* and you're going to take a fall.

Marui isn't something exclusive to the ways of fighting. It's part and parcel of Japanese life. For example, there's a lot of it in the Japanese style of conversation. Where we like to "get right to the point," as when a supervisor gives feedback to a subordinate, or when friends ask you what you *really* think of them and you tell them directly and in no uncertain terms, the Japanese prefer to talk around a subject. They move in a series of conversational rings, getting closer to the "point" when they think the listener is ready and able to understand and accept it, and moving away from it when the timing isn't so right.

The indirect approach grew out of the ancient concepts of *wa* and *ai*. Each is still a key feature of Oriental life. *Wa* means accord or cooperation. It is achieved by blending with things and life generally, or in the martial ways by blending your counterattack with your opponent's attack. *Ai* means "harmony," or "to unite." Ai-ki-do literally means the way (do) of harmonizing (ai) your spirit (ki) with your opponent's; making your spirit "fit in" with your enemy's and bringing your movements into accord with his. The *aikidoka* "serves" the attacker by being sensitive to his needs and intentions.

Since all indirect fighting styles exploit your opponents' power, the more aggressive they are, the more they play into your hands and the easier they are to control. That's very important to remember. When your opponent comes charging at you with a full head of steam, you have more power to work with than when someone sidles up tentatively. All that matters in a fight situation is your being able to use the total power that's there, yours and your opponent's. When you use the judo approach, you apply the principle of "five plus five is ten; two plus eight is ten," *go-go ju, ni-hachi ju:* when your opponent pushes with five units of power, pull with five units of power; the result is ten units. When he (or she) pulls with eight units, push with two units; the result is still ten. The more they supply, the less you have to supply. Who appears to have power isn't the important thing. What matters is who actually has *control* of it.

Examples of Using Power Indirectly

You can demonstrate to yourself that yielding to an opponent's force to gain your objective is not totally alien to the West.

• *Sports.* The next time you're watching a football game, keep your eyes on an experienced defensive lineman. Most of the time he'll charge into the opposing lineman, force against force; but at other times he'll roll off him, spin around and then dash through a hole in the line. That's *marui.*

• *Selling.* The bottom-line task of all business is creating a customer. Effectiveness always boils down to selling. Many a huge corporation is being carried on the backs of a small group of salespeople who consistently out-sell the competition. What are these high-producers like? How do they operate? Look at them closely and you see that they're indirect power users. They're the *aikidokas* and *judokas* of the business world.

Study after study shows that the most effective salesmen and women handle their prospect's objections in a particular way. When the prospect raises an objection, the highly effective salesman doesn't resist it. Instead, he "goes with it" in the judo way. He does this by repeating or paraphrasing the objection. "I see what you mean, Mr. Smith. You want to be very sure that we can deliver a load of steel to you on time." By handling the objection this way rather than avoiding it or trying to beat it down, the salesman is giving the prospect exactly what he wants— recognition that he has a concern that is personally important to him. The effective salesman, like the *aikidoka*, understands the other person's intentions and then goes *with* them. He makes use of resistance, he doesn't oppose it. After responding to the objection with more information he then continues the presentation.

• *Conversational persuasion.* Two professors of speech from New York University listened to more than ten thousand "arguments"—between taxi drivers and their fares, salesmen and prospects, diplomats at the United Nations, etc. Those who attempted to hammer an opponent down with tough, powerful arguments did not succeed in changing the other person's mind. The most successful were salesmen who didn't try to win the argument or to force the opponent to change, but used calm logic to change the prospect's mind.

• *Retailing.* The Marshall Field department store in Chicago became a world-famous retailer when it developed a policy of *wa* or *ai*, which it embodied in the memorable motto "Give the lady what she wants."

The indirect use of power is considerably more than an interesting alternative to direct force-against-force power moves. It is a *daido*, a broad principle with practical applications not only to military combat, but to all areas of human existence, including corporate life. Whenever there is a disagreement between two people—springing from differences in their idea of what will best serve their own self-interest—a direct power attack from either person will tend to generate rigid resistance in the other. Manager/subordinate, salesperson/prospect, marketing director/production manager, union representative/industrial relations director, and customer relations staff/customer are examples of points of conflict which are commonly found in business enterprises.

Although at times the direct use of power may help you convert the other person to your opinion, the process of overcoming the resistance, which your force has created, will often be arduous and time-consuming. Agreement to your view is far more easily and quickly reached by turning resistance aside *marui*, "circular motion" style, or by rolling with it in a judo fashion.

The indirect style was used by Andrew Carnegie, one of our greatest businessmen. The boom period of the railroad industry in the latter part of the nineteenth century saw the emergence of the railroad sleeping car. At the time there were two major firms competing in the field, Carnegie and Westinghouse. Carnegie, ever a shrewd businessman, realized there were more profits to be made by joining interests with Westinghouse than by competing. Carnegie made the overture, but Westinghouse at first was cool to the idea. Gradually, though, Westinghouse became interested and met with Carnegie to talk it over. Suddenly Westinghouse blurted out, "But what is the new firm to be called?" Without missing a beat, Carnegie replied, "Westinghouse, naturally." "Done," said Westinghouse, and that was that. A Masamune man in action.

The customer relations representative who after listening to a complaint expresses a "tough luck, take it or leave it" attitude is not going to be remotely as successful in keeping that customer as the one who starts with "You're absolutely right," or "If that happened to me I'd feel just like you," or "We really blew it. We owe you . . ."

In an attempt to gain ground against Johnson & Johnson's Tylenol, Bristol-Myers offered a less expensive product, Datril, and planned a hard-hitting advertising campaign focusing on cost. Johnson & Johnson defeated Bristol-Myers by going with the cost issue. They simply went indirect and lowered Tylenol's price.

Samurai general Nagauji Hojo (1432–1519) advised his son, "Be careful of pushing through your personal opinion." Nobushige of the great Takeda warrior family added, "Good medicine tastes bitter but fights the disease. Words uttered in good faith may hurt, but improve one's conduct." Time and again the consultative style of management (discussing problems with subordinates before making the final decisions) has been shown to produce the highest-quality business and industrial performance. Will a manager be successful if he is given to blaming, ridiculing, chiding and chastising? Probably half the open-door policies in this country are never taken advantage of by even one employee because behind the desk beyond the open door sat a direct-power-using Muramasa.

Implicit in the so-called "trait" or "great man" theory of leadership was the belief that the leader was one who imposed his will, goals and values on those below him—by force if necessary. It is widely recognized today that such a perception of the leader's role does not hold up. The effective leader is the one who recognizes the interests held dear by subordinates and unleashes commitment not by opposing or supplanting those interests but by going with them, by strengthening them.

Hart Schaffner & Marx, Kelly Services (Kelly Girls) and Montgomery Ward are examples of businesses that went with customers' ideas and prospered because of it. Hart Schaffner & Marx was a small clothing store which as a sideline manufactured a few high-quality suits for preferred customers. It was only after one customer suggested that manufacturing should be the *real* business that the store owners researched the idea and discovered the customer was right.

When Russell Kelly founded Kelly Services he believed that his business was in bringing typing and duplicating work from neighboring companies into his offices. When one accountant requested temporary help in his own office, Kelly yielded to the idea. He quickly saw that outstationing his "girls" on an as-needed basis was his *real* business.

Montgomery Ward was strictly a mail-order house which held merchandise exhibits throughout the country merely to show buyers the items described in the MW catalogue. The items on display were not for sale—until, that is, one stubborn farmer would not take no for an answer. He had seen a product on display and wanted it *then*, without waiting for delivery. The MW display manager, obviously an indirect power user, approved the sale. He also put *all* the display merchandise up for sale. Word spread quickly and every item was sold. Taking an indirect, "going-with" approach, Ward's quickly went into the over-the-counter business and in short order opened hundreds of outlets across the country.

Extending

"We're number two. We try harder."
Avis Rent A Car

"Extending" is a crucial concept of force in aikido. It means bringing your opponent's movement a little beyond its natural point of conclusion, leaving him in an off-balance position. You help the attacker go in the direction he wishes to go, but *farther* in the direction than he expects. If you are an "extending" salesman you will not stop at repeating or paraphrasing the prospect's objection, but will exaggerate it. "I think you're saying that you want us to make sure the steel is delivered to your docks three or four months before you actually need it for production." Now you know the prospect means no such thing. But you also know, sometimes intuitively, that when you exaggerate the prospect's objections an interesting thing often happens. *The prospect deflates his own objection.*

"Well, no, I'm not asking for delivery that far ahead of time. All I'm asking is that we have the stuff a reasonable period in advance."

Business meetings in America often involve the very direct use of power. One person confronts and attacks another. It's off to the force-against-force races. If you're more powerful you beat me down, but if the reverse is true you're in trouble. The same is true in meetings of all types —of politicians, condominium owners, PTAs, boards of charities, etc. In contrast, Japanese meetings generally utilize the approach of never directly confronting or clashing with the other person, and that is the reason why cooperative harmony is so noticeable in Japanese business.

End results of confrontations are often battered feelings, anger, defensiveness, lowered morale and a desire for retribution. The aikido businessman, like the effective salesman, would not oppose his power to the other's power, but offering little resistance to the assault would guide the energetic power thrust in directions more useful to him.

BOSS: "The situation in your department is very bad."

YOU: "I agree with you. It's very bad. *It might even be hopeless.*"

BOSS: "Well, I wouldn't go that far. It's bad, but there are things we can do about it."

YOU: "Maybe you're right. There probably are things we can do about it."

BOSS: "Sure I'm right."

In a matter of seconds you've turned a potentially explosive force-against-force situation into a cooperative one. And you've done it by extending, by exaggerating your agreement . . .

Now let's move out of the business meeting and into the privacy of your own home.

WIFE: "Damn it, you didn't take the trash out again."

YOU: (Instead of blasting her with "Trash is the least of my worries!") "You're right. I didn't. I feel bad about it. I know it's inconvenient for you, tripping over it. I'm sorry."

WIFE: "Well, I don't want to make you feel bad. I'd just like to make
sure it's taken out."

Once again you have achieved the fighter's ideal of avoiding conflict.
By making the choice not to strike back, you have turned what could
have been a fierce domestic force-against-force skirmish into a spirit of
harmony (ai).

You demonstrated consideration for the wife's point of view ("I know
it's inconvenient for you . . .") and she, who was angry and *against* you
a short moment earlier, is now with you ("I don't want to make you feel
bad.") And she has still gotten her point across—the trash has to be
taken out.

What happened in this example is exactly what samurai master of the
sword Tsuji meant when he wrote, "When you reach real ability you will
be able to become one with the enemy. Entering his heart you will see
that he is not your enemy after all."

Another technique of effective salesmanship blends direct and indirect approaches. For example, imagine yourself trying to sell a prospect
on buying something. All during your presentation the prospect has been
negative toward your product. He's found a hundred and one reasons
why it wouldn't be right for him. You've tried your darndest to answer all
his objections and questions, but to no avail. You feel you've done a good
job, but he's still stone-cold to buying. You're at a choice point here. You
could continue to hammer away, providing more and more information,
but your sense is that he still won't buy. So instead, you suddenly agree
with him. You go indirect and extend.

Suddenly close your order book, purse your lips and say something
like, "Mr. Jones, I've been thinking it over and I've decided that I can't
in good conscience sell you this product." Then add something that will
get him to want to sell *you* on selling it to him. Such as, "For one thing I
don't know if you can afford it on your salary."

You're at a strategic point now. If Jones is like most people he will give
you a reason why he could afford it.

"Well I'm not exactly a pauper, you know. We're only talking about a
few hundred dollars."

"You're right, Mr. Jones. It's not much money. But frankly, most of
our buyers are in a slightly higher bracket."

"You're not saying I couldn't buy it, are you?"

"Oh no, I'm only saying that I wouldn't want you to buy it if you can't afford it."

"I can afford it."

"Maybe you're right. Let's see how we could work it out."

Few battles are won by extending only once. With Jones you might have to do it two, three or four times. Keep extending and you'll get what you want more often than not.

It's no secret that many prospects have a hard time making up their minds. You've been talking with one like this for some time and have tried the direct approach of making him decide right then and there, but without success. If you shift into the indirect, "going with" approach you might have better results.

Once again, break the action. Let the prospect know you've thought the situation over. Then say something like, "Mr. Smith, a lot of people are able to make a decision right off the bat and stick by it, but a few others need to check it out with somebody else. To tell you the truth, I wouldn't want to sell you something before you've received their permission."

All along Smith has been telling you in one way or another that someone else's decision is more important than his. But when you present it to him this way he probably is going to want to show you he's not indecisive and he doesn't need to get someone else's permission.

The indirect, extending approach has also been used to resolve potential labor-management problems. Koichi Tsukamoto is President of Japan's Wacoal Corporation, a manufacturer of women's clothes. In 1962 a trade union was established in Wacoal, and soon labor-management relations were poor. Deeply disturbed by the chasm of distrust between the company and workers, Tsukamoto tried to figure out what to do to bring the sides together. He decided that the only way would be to *trust* his workers. But he realized just saying it to them wasn't enough. He had to show them.

He settled on new policies. One was that being late for work, quitting early or leaving for personal reasons was to be left totally to the workers. Time clocks were taken down and thrown away. Another policy was an even more important demonstration of his trust in the workers. *Whatever demands the union committee drew up would be accepted completely and automatically, one hundred percent.*

When he presented his decision to his board of directors they were horrified. They said the company would go bankrupt. He told them it might, but if it came to that, then they would just have to go bankrupt, but something had to be done to close the gap with the workers. Tsukamoto met with groups of five to ten workers at a time and emphasized to them that the new policies were not intended to make workers trust him, but to let them know he trusted them.

The union representatives came to him with their demands. Without even looking at them he put his seal on them just as he had promised.

"Are the demands okay?" asked one representative. After reading them, Tsukamoto said that since the union had been formed worker productivity had been only 40 percent and that if it continued the company would go broke. He said he thought that if productivity reached 80 percent the company would prosper.

And that is exactly what happened. The workers doubled their productivity and the company prospered. Koichi says the policy of automatic agreement is still in effect, and will be as long as there is a Wacoal. Has there been any labor trouble since?

"Never," says Tsukamoto.

Avis Rent A Car extended itself right into huge profits. For thirteen years it hid the fact it wasn't *numero uno* and each year lost money. Then it stopped hiding it and started advertising the fact. The next year Avis made $1.2 million, the next year double that and the following year double *that*.

No doubt you have had people consume an hour reciting all the reasons why they can't solve a particular problem. Why argue with them? Instead, extend: "You know, I think you're right. There's absolutely no way under the sun you'll be able to solve this one. There's *nothing* you can do." Wait five seconds while they get over their shock, and they will say "What do you mean? There are plenty of things I can do. I could always . . ."

Do the same thing whenever you are telling yourself that you can't solve a problem, and the result will be the same.

Teachers, too, can benefit from learning the strategic value of extending, of going with rather than meeting force with force. A grade school teacher I know was having a lot of trouble with a boy who bothered the other students, jabbered incessantly and started fights. The teacher was going crazy trying to figure out what to do with (or to) him. At first she thought of suspending him from class or having him dismissed. But instead she simply asked him more questions during class and sought his help with chores around the room. Immediately there was a complete turnaround in his behavior. Why? Because she had given him precisely what his misbehavior had been a request for, what he "intended" to get—her personal attention. All he wanted was to be noticed, to be singled out. She helped him to achieve what he wanted in a constructive way by not opposing him.

I conduct business seminars across the country. My experience is not very different from that teacher's. Every once in a while I encounter people who at the beginning of a seminar are disruptive in one way or another. Instead of meeting the force of their disruption with the force of a "Damn it, will you shut up," I use the indirect extending approach. At the first coffee break I pull them aside and tell them I need them. I try to give them what everyone needs but what disruptors need more than others—personal, individual recognition. I ask for their help in making the program successful. And they always give it.

When I was seventeen, having graduated from high school and needing money for college, I got a job in a factory. Like everyone else I brought my brown bag and left it on a rack in a storeroom. One day when we went to eat, the bag with my name on it was missing. I asked around and nobody knew anything. The next day the same thing happened. On the third day I made two lunches, wrote my name on one and "FOR THE THIEF" in huge letters on the other, and placed them side by side on the rack. When I came in to get my lunch both bags were still there. I never had my lunch stolen after that.

Behind your opponent's attack lies something deep, and it's this that you're trying to redirect when you use the indirect, extending approach. It's the opponent's intention to do battle with you. If you can eliminate that there won't be any fight. If you simply refuse to participate there cannot be a battle. In business and private life alike there are all too many opportunities for conflict. If you realize that a confrontation is headed your way, try to react in a way that will defuse the other person's anger. Or simply let your opponents be angry if they wish. You might feel like striking back, especially if you're a Muramasa, but resist the feeling. Let their anger come out but don't give any back. This isn't being a martyr. It's just achieving the samurai ideal of winning the fight without fighting. You'll see victory come your way when, with no one to fight, your opponent simply stops attacking.

Emotional Aikido:
Extending with Your Inner Opponents

We've seen that the strategic principle of the indirect use of power—don't oppose force, but extend your opponent's power thrust—can be applied successfully to an outer opponent. It can also be used to win out over your inner opponents—a kind of emotional aikido.

All your emotions are forms of energy. Each and every one of your emotions is power. Your positive feelings of excitement, pleasure, joy, courage, optimism, confidence and love can fill your actions with an almost unbelievable power. You know that yourself without even having to think twice about it. When you're filled with really positive feelings there's hardly anything you feel you cannot do. Hardly anything can stop you.

Your negative emotions are also power. But they're destructive. Your fear, worry, anxiety, depression, anger, nervousness and all the other inner dragons are power that's being used in the wrong way. It's energy that's pointed in the wrong direction. It's directed inward, *against* you. It holds you back. It keeps you down.

Emotional aikido is a way of transforming negative, inward-directed emotional power into positive power pointed outward. It transforms your harmful emotions into helpful ones, and it does so by *going with* your harmful emotions, not opposing them.

Neurologist Dr. Viktor Frankl points out that, paradoxically, trying too hard at something often makes it impossible. For example, the person who is afraid of blushing and *tries hard not to* when he enters a room full of people will actually blush. The person who is afraid of stuttering and *tries hard not to* will stutter. Frankl calls this "hyper" intention. It's intending too much and too hard. A classic example of too much intending is the man who is so damned intent on impressing his partner with his sexual prowess that he tries too hard and fails miserably.

Frankl realized that hyper-intending could be a very useful way to rid people of emotional impediments: If a person stuttered when he tried very hard not to, wouldn't he be unable to stutter if he tried very hard to make himself stutter? And that's exactly what happened. A man with a lifelong severe case of stuttering stopped only when he tried very hard to force himself to stutter. A man who had suffered from writer's cramp for some years was cured by trying not to write neatly and legibly, but in the worst possible scrawl. The moment he deliberately tried to scribble, he couldn't. Using the technique of hyper-intention, Dr. Frankl even cured a healthy man of his terrifying fear of having a heart attack. He had him try to induce one! The man worked at it like the devil. He huffed and puffed trying to make it happen. What happened was that the heart attack didn't, but the man lost his irrational fear of one.

In going into battle against a disturbing inner emotion you have a choice to make. If you're a direct force-against-force stylist you'll probably attempt to overcome the emotion directly through willpower. You'll tell yourself, "I won't let this thing get the better of me. I will not blush this time . . . will not stammer . . . will not feel nervous, afraid, worried, depressed," etc., etc., etc.

According to Frankl, that approach only increases the problem: "Pressure precipitates counter-pressure." But if you use the indirect, extending style of hyper-intention you stand a far better chance. To use it, you (1) take the frontal approach by identifying the emotion that's disturbing you, and then you (2) go with it and exaggerate it. If you're feeling afraid of something tell yourself things that will make you even more afraid. Fear your guts out. Fear to beat the band. Do the same thing for any feeling that's troubling you. All your emotions have a saturation point which when reached will stop the emotion. Emotional extending is over-saturating them.

You can't ignore the worries, fears and anxieties that get in your way and interfere with your functioning and feeling well, just as you cannot ignore any opponent without risking defeat. They're *real*. They're blocking you. And to win you have no choice but to deal with them. You can't will them out of existence by pitting your willpower against their power. But you can extend them out of existence. Don't attempt to suppress them or beat them down. Do the opposite—exaggerate them, hyper-intend them, over-saturate them, extend them.

Guidelines for Making Your Power Decisions

• Begin with the insight that to defeat your opponents you must (1) use your power and (2) use it effectively. If you constantly find yourself crawling back home or to your desk to lick your wounds; if you're continually assaulted by deep shame, fierce anger and bitter outrage, it's probably because you're refusing to use your power at all or you're using it ineffectively.

• Appraise your habitual power style. Generally speaking, are you more of a Muramasa "let's duke it out" stylist or are you more of a Masamune "We can work this out without fighting" person?

If you're more Muramasa, you are no doubt spending an inordinate amount of your time fighting needlessly. I confess to having been one of the most blatant Muramasas you'll probably ever encounter. Here's a technique I learned to use. It's called *Imagine a Ring*.

As I mentioned in Chapter 4, you can avoid many fights by imagining a ring of cooperation encircling yourself and your potential opponent or opponents. Actually visualize the two or more of you ringed in by a brightly colored circle. Say to yourself that no matter what goes on outside this circle, inside it there will be cooperation and goodwill. If there are disagreements inside this circle, you can work them out. Turn your power into a spirit of cooperation. Conflicts are merely temporary disruptions of harmony. If you're inside the circle they can be resolved. Masamune people live in circles of cooperation, whether they're managers, salespeople, marketers, housewives, auditors, labor negotiators or entrepreneurs. Whoever they are and whatever they do, their first expectation is that there isn't going to be a fight. And usually there isn't.

• Select the way of using your power that will serve you and the situation best. Whenever you reach a power decision point—with a sales prospect, an employee or anyone—say to yourself, "I have a choice here. I could go direct, force-against-force with this person (or emotion), or I could go indirect and extend. Which way is best in this particular situation?"

The direct approach works effectively in "kill" situations when you are far more powerful than your opponent is, have no reason to fear retribution and have no need of the other person's willing cooperation in the future—conditions not often met in business or social life.

• If you choose to use the indirect approach, be sensitive to your opponent's intentions. The way to "serve" one's opponents in the aikido style is to understand what they want, and to give them more of it to get what *you* want.

If the "intention" of your fear is to make you feel afraid, give it what it wants. Make yourself feel *more* afraid.

What do people generally want in any human interaction? Respect, recognition, individual attention, to be liked, to be listened to. Always give them what they want. The law of social reciprocation says: Give people something of value and they will want to give you something of value in return.

When you use your power in the direct force-against-force way, you view your opponent's *personality* as a target of your attack or counterattack: "I'll show this bozo a thing or two." But using power indirectly, his personality is not a target, but an aid to you. If he's the kind who likes to embarrass people, tell him you're *very* embarrassed. Figure out the effect he wants to work on you and let him know he's succeeded—exaggerate your reactions.

• Whatever you do, don't mistake the indirect, extending approach for bland Caspar Milquetoast surrender. It's a mistake many Westerners make when they try "going Eastern." The indirect approach is not at all the same as letting yourself get stepped on, walked over, hammered and mauled. It is an incredibly effective way of using the total power in any situation—yours *and* your opponent's.

Most Americans have been conditioned not to be indirect extenders. We have been taught that the best way to win anything is to go toe-to-toe with our adversaries, our dukes up, ready to punch it out with them. Most of us have to learn for ourselves that at times it's more productive to be like the aikidoka and to roll with the punches our outer or inner opponents throw.

Study the examples in this chapter, then practice extending at work, at home, at restaurants, grocery stores, banks, with customers and negative emotions. In particular, whenever you find yourself at loggerheads with any opponent, inner or outer, and you realize that you can't advance, "soak in" as Musashi says, "and become one with the enemy."

9

Identifying *Suki*, the Gap

"You've reached the wisdom of strategy
when you cannot be deceived by men."

Musashi Miyamoto, swordsman

Gunpaisha in Business; Gunpaisha in You

Knowing which strategy to use and when and how to use it is one of your most important fighting skills. If you're losing a lot of your battles in *any* area of life—being interviewed for a job, asking for a date, running a corporation or managing your career—it might be that you're using the wrong strategy. Or you may be using the right one in the wrong way or at the wrong time.

In samurai combat the supreme masters of strategy—the brains of the outfit—were called *gunpaisha,* or "keepers of *gunpai,*" large metal fans which were carried into battle and on which was inscribed information pertinent to the conduct of the battle. We have our own *gunpaisha* in corporate life. We call them long-range planners, marketing and advertising strategists and product researchers. Warfare is their game, and like their samurai counterparts they must be thoroughly familiar with its techniques.

There's a *gunpaisha*-strategist in you too. If he's any good he's a key element of your success in any of your battles—in business and outside it, and against your outer as well as your inner opponents.

Two Strategies

Attack or counterattack—these are the two strategies the samurai used, and you use them too. The strategy of attack, *ken no sen*, is launching an assault before your opponent's attack is launched against you. In samurai fighting the attack strategy is also called "the lead of the lead." It's winning by taking the lead and hanging on to it.

Using the second strategy—counterattack—you wait until your opponent attacks you, and then you swing into your fighting response. It's called *tai no sen*, "to wait for the initiative" or "the lead of reaction." When your opponents attack, you counter with a defensive action to stop or neutralize them, then snatch the lead away from them.

Every striking technique or *waza* of samurai swordsmanship follows from attack or counterattack strategies. *Shikake-waza* are offensive attack techniques; *oji-waza*, "receiving techniques," are applications of counterattack strategy. Chapter 10, *"Waza:* Techniques for Striking Your Opponent," concentrates on *waza*. That chapter and this one are close companions.

The strategy of *ken no sen* attack is the bolder of the two. It takes guts. It's seizing the initiative and using surprise and speed to your advantage. It was the chief strategy of the *ninja*, those extraordinary exponents of stealth, and it was the strategic style swordsman Musashi liked best. In kendo it's also called the "positive style." Attack, "lead of the lead" and the positive style all mean the same thing: defeating your opponents through relentless, devastating attacks that confuse them, force them into making a mistake or catch them with their guard down.

There's no doubt that if you're an attack, lead-of-the-lead, positive-style person you can win many of your fights. But there are arguments against being the first to launch an attack. It might be the bolder strategy but not necessarily the more effective one.

The main drawback to attacking first is your vulnerability as your move develops. The results of your attack can be totally devastating to an adversary who is weak or unprepared. But if you're attacking a powerful and alert opponent, you're exposing yourself to counterattack at every step, particularly between the point of beginning your move and reaching your full strength.

Because of the vulnerability factor, most martial artists prefer the counterattack. The next time you see a karate tournament on television, notice how neither fighter really wants to attack. The action of the fight lies in its flurry of counterattacks.

The so-called "vacant style" in kendo is a counterattack strategy. The heart of the vacant style is *suki o mitsukeru.* You rivet your attention on your opponent and with lightning speed take advantage of any opening in his defense. The vacant style could just as well be called the patient style, because you need extraordinary patience to wait for your opponent to make a false move or a blunder.

Some people are superb counterattackers. They're just terrific at waiting for their opponents to take the initiative and then taking it away from them. In business meetings it may mean drawing out your opponents and getting them to lay their cards on the table. You just sit back and keep your eyes and ears open while they attack. Then, when the right time comes, you use what you've seen and heard in your counterattack.

In sales this strategy means listening attentively while prospective buyers declare themselves, telling you what their objections are, what questions they have and what benefits they're interested in. Once you've heard them, you go into action to answer questions, respond to objections and hammer away at the benefits you've been told directly or indirectly are most important.

If you're a sales person using *ken no sen* attack strategy you do most of the talking. Instead of asking the prospect if he or she has a question or reservations about buying, *you* raise questions and objections which the prospect might have. Then you respond to them with positive, factual information. Instead of asking, "Do you have any questions?" to set up your counterattack, you say "You're probably wondering about price. Well, you'll be happy to hear . . ."

Ken no sen attack in establishing a salary for the job you've applied for is stating what your requirements are without finding out what the salary offer is. *Tai no sen* counterattack is discovering what the offer is before naming any specific figure.

Whenever you use *attack* strategies in business or personal life, you declare your position before the other person does: "This is what I want to do; this is my opinion on the matter; this is how I see it; here's how I'm going to go with this . . ."

Counterattack is based on holding back and not committing yourself to your move until you learn what your opponents want, what their opinion is, how they see it or how they intend to proceed.

Whether using attack or counterattack, you are aware of what you want. The difference is *when* you divulge that information to the other person.

Selling any kind of personalized service is counterattack business. It's a total waste of time to try to convince prospects that they need a service you have to offer. A far better approach is to feel them out. Let them tell you what the need is, then sell them on your ability to fill it.

Japanese business is counterattack business, as is Japanese culture generally. The highest skill of the Japanese company is not so much developing new products, but refining products already developed by someone else (the attacker), then manufacturing them more inexpensively and offering them to the consumer at lower prices. The Japanese prefer to let someone else absorb the high costs of research and development.

In fact, though, the choice of your fighting strategy is not a matter of which, but when. To do really well in fighting of any kind you have to be able to attack *and* counterattack. The principle of *kobo-itchi* is a very important one in samurai fighting. It states that the choice of strategy depends on the situation. Great fighters not only can attack and counterattack, but can do both with excellence. Even if you're a wonderful attacker you're going to have problems when your opponent is an even better counterattacker. And even if you're absolutely whiz-bang at the counterattack, you're not going to have an opportunity to show it if your adversary simply refuses to attack. To be a master fighter in any field you must be able to shift flexibly from attack to counterattack, from counterattack to attack and back—whether you're a swordsman, negotiator, teacher, psychotherapist, businessman or anything else.

Suki: the Gap

The August 1954 race between Roger Bannister of England and Australia's John Landy, the so-called "mile of the century," was one of the most memorable of all time. There have been other "miles of the century" since, but none as dramatic as this one in Vancouver.

Landy was leading down the home stretch when he committed the cardinal sin of looking back! He glanced over his left shoulder. In that fraction of a second, the alert Bannister burst past him on the right. Bannister's reaction was so instantaneous and explosive, his timing so perfect, that he was passing Landy at the precise moment when the Australian could not possibly see him. Landy didn't realize he had been passed until he turned his head frontward and saw the tall Englishman ahead of him. Bannister won the race by five yards.

This incident illustrates a key concept in samurai fighting: *Suki.* Literally *suki* means a space between two objects where something else can enter, a slit or crack. In fighting it's an interval of relaxation, a gap in the fighter's attention. It's an unguarded moment, however slight, or an opening that you can take advantage of. Landy's *suki* was that split-second glance over his left shoulder.

If you have ever lifted heavy weights you have experienced *suki* when your concentration was suddenly taken off the lift. Someone calls you, or your thoughts drift to something else. What happens? The very moment you relax your concentration, you lose power and the weight starts to slip. What caused the power loss was that interval of mental relaxation, that *suki.* In baseball *suki* happens when the player takes his eyes off the ball.

It occurs when you're fighting inner opponents too, as when you become depressed or discouraged. The moment you do, your enthusiasm and self-confidence fly out the window. Inner dragons are caused by inner *suki.* A gap opens and the negatives of fear, depression, anger, hesitation and self-doubt come rushing in to fill it.

Understanding *suki* is really the backbone of marketing. A useful marketing plan begins with the identification of trends in the marketplace that the company can take advantage of. Coca-Cola developed Fresca because it clearly saw and took advantage of a *suki* gap in the marketplace: consumers were interested in good-tasting dietetic drinks. Ford, on the other hand, completely ignored a possible *suki* gap—a consumer desire for lower-priced cars—and tried to peddle the bigger, more expensive Edsel. Knowing your consumer like the back of your hand is the key to marketing success, just as knowing your opponent inside and out is a key to victory in fighting.

In business, *suki* is often revealed when you see something your competitors don't see. Their blindness is their *suki*. For example, Thomas Bata was a Slovakian who visited the United States after World War I. Being a shoemaker, Bata was struck by the fact that here everybody had shoes, whereas in his own country the peasants didn't. If you were poor, it was just taken for granted you went barefoot. Upon his return to Europe, using what he had seen in America, Bata developed affordable, mass-produced but high-quality shoes, something none of his competitors had ever thought about doing. Within just a few years he ran Europe's largest shoe manufacturing concern and one of the continent's most successful businesses.

Two questions for you: Why is *suki* such an important concept in samurai fighting? And why is it that you will reach more victories as soon as you acquire the habit of spotting *suki* in your opponents and even in yourself?

For two reasons. One, because—

> Whether you choose the attack or counterattack
> strategy, your objective is always the same—
> your opponent's *suki*.

The style of relentless, aggressive, lead-of-the-lead *ken no sen* attack is designed to *create suki* in your opponent. You hit hard and force your adversary into making an error in judgment. It's the hard-hitting German blitzkrieg of World War II, or the blitz in football.

The purpose of the *tai no sen* counterattack style, on the other hand, is not to create *suki* in your opponent, but to spot it and then take advantage of it. It's the perceptive quarterback reading the blitz and letting the defense rush madly in before softly dropping off a screen pass to his running back.

And two, because—

> If you're losing a lot of your fights it's
> because *your suki* are leaving you wide open.

It's not by coincidence that "samurai" means "to be on guard." When assuming the *seiza* sitting-kneeling position the samurai always knelt with his left knee first. When rising he always moved the right first. Why? So that he was always in a position to quickly draw his sword, which he carried on his left side. As he bowed at the threshold of a house he held an iron fan in each hand next to his head to prevent the sliding doors being used as a vise to clamp his head. One samurai gives this advice: "Even when alone with his wife, the samurai should not forget to keep his sword at hand."

You don't have to go to those extremes, but do be on guard against your own *suki*—the cracks, gaps, holes and slits in your own fighting style, your way of operating, even your way of thinking—and try to cut them down to a minimum. They're bringing you defeat, so get rid of them.

Keeping a Book

If you know your opponent and you know yourself,
    you will always win;
If you don't know your opponent, but you know
    yourself, you will win only half the time;
If you know neither your opponent nor yourself
    you will always lose.

Samurai maxim

To spot *suki* in others—consumers, competitors, a stranger at a party you want to impress, someone who's interviewing you for a job—you need information on them. That's all there is to it.

How do you acquire that information for your own *gunpai* battle fan? One method is acquiring it before the battle. I call that "keeping a book." The other is more typically samurai, and more typical in business and personal life—using the action itself to pick up the information. It's "counting your opponent's rifles."

It's amazing how often you know what your close friends are thinking and how each of them will react under various circumstances. You know what their intentions are, their strengths and weaknesses and how they handle themselves. You know what gets their goat, their hot buttons and tender spots. It is exactly this type of *suki* knowledge that the skilled businessman possesses about his opponent. Your adversaries may be your worst enemies and you may even hate them, but the more you know them the way you know a dear friend the better you'll be at defeating them. Musashi calls it "becoming" the enemy. It's the *gunpaisha* art of thinking yourself into the enemy's position. You see it often in sports, as suggested by these remarks of base stealer *extraordinaire* Lou Brock: "So you try to make that pitcher your very close buddy, by empathizing with all his moves and all his thoughts. You know at one point he has to commit himself, and that he can't go back on it." However you acquire the information, the kind you want is the type that will enable you to "become" your opponent.

When sports teams scout their opponents and study game films, their *gunpaisha* coaches are looking for the other team's *suki*. Outdoorsmen do the same thing. Having "scouted" the salmon, the fisherman knows that the salmon's *suki* is his instinct, which makes him return to the lake where he was born. If you're the fisherman and you want to catch salmon, just put salmon eggs in the lake of your choice, then sit back and wait for the full-grown fish to come home after going downstream to mature.

In baseball, pitchers keep a "book" on batters. The book records the pitches the pitcher has used successfully against the batter, and the hitter's strengths and weaknesses, or *suki*. Batters do the same. Stan Musial catalogued and memorized *each* of the pitches thrown by every pitcher in the National League.

Like the baseball player, the master samurai kept a book on his prospective adversaries. Master Azato, a famous *karateka*, maintained a file of highly detailed information on the abilities, skills, techniques, strengths and weaknesses of all experts he was ever likely to come up against.

In international politics, "books" are kept on national leaders. The purpose of the book is to predict the leader's future decisions from past tendencies. Former President Carter reports that reading Menachem Begin's autobiography, *The Revolt,* immediately before the Camp David conference contributed directly to the successful completion of the Israeli-Egyptian peace accord. Before his first meeting with Soviet Premier Khrushchev, President Kennedy made a thorough study of the Premier's life and of his speeches and positions on various matters, and even made it a point to familiarize himself with Khrushchev's tastes in food and music.

Like sports teams, fishermen, baseball players, diplomats, samurai and presidents, before you go into battle you too will want to scout your opponents and identify their *suki*—if it's possible. You'll want to keep a book on them. At times your book will be an actual set of written comments on your opponents. At other times it will not be written down at all, but will just consist of a few ideas you have about them.

At times your book, your *gunpai*, is a fat one, chock-full of information. And sometimes the information is skimpy, but nonetheless useful.

When I Discovered *Suki* in the Other Team's Star

Since our high school didn't have its own outdoor track, my teammate Tony and I practiced on a track some distance from our school. On this particular day, the track was also being used by a team we were going to compete against in two days. When the team's coach learned that Tony was to run the mile, he introduced us to his own miler, Ken, the star of their team.

Tony's objective that day was to run a hard three miles, and mine was to begin with Tony, drop out after a mile, then concentrate on a series of 220s to develop my speed. Tony was an unusual runner. He couldn't run a particularly fast mile, but he could keep his mile pace up for three miles. He was a pretty good miler, but a *great* three-miler.

As planned, I dropped out after a mile and Tony continued running a very fine three miles. While I was actually faster than Tony in all events, his appearance was more imposing. He was much taller, long-legged and stronger. I was a skinny runt.

When our team appeared at the meet I learned that Ken had decided not to run against Tony, but had chosen instead to run against me in the half-mile. As always, I tried to figure out what my opponent's weaknesses were. I didn't know about *suki* then, but that's exactly what I was looking for. Since I'd never run against Ken before, I had very little to go on. My *gunpai* had just about nothing inscribed on it. But I had *something*, and it didn't take a genius to figure out what it was. All I had to do was ask myself why Ken had decided to leave his regular event to come down to mine. The answer seemed obvious: Ken was scared of Tony! Tony's strong distance running and physical appearance had shaken Ken's confidence, and so he had decided he would rather run against me, the puny guy, the "easier" competition.

Normally my running strategy was counterattack. I would hang back about five yards behind the leader and count on the speed of my finishing kick to carry me to victory.

Intimidation is a battle of wills, and I decided that was Ken's *suki:* you could beat him by attacking his will. I decided to do this, or at least try, by completely changing my strategy—by blasting off the starting line and running him into the ground, relying on my will to defeat his by being able to endure more pain.

In the race I *saw* Ken's will snap. We were running at a furious pace, a ridiculous pace. I remember hearing my coach screaming, "Rogers, what the hell are you doing?" After one lap the pain caught up with Ken and he dropped out. Immediately I slowed down and struggled through the last lap in agony, but won. Later that afternoon Ken was scheduled to run the anchor of the mile relay against me. Before the event, he asked the coach if he could run the third leg instead. He never again entered a race I was also in.

Counting Rifles

"The warrior works his way to victory in relation to his foe."
Sonshi

With Ken I was fortunate to have learned what his *suki* was before going into battle with him. I had a kind of book on him before we stepped to the starting line. That's the ideal situation for the fighter, but it's often not possible in your business or personal life. Usually the situation isn't very clearcut. Often you have precious little information, or none at all. You just don't know what your opponent's *suki* is.

Going in cold, without a clear sense of strategy or *suki*, occurs frequently in business, as when your associate asks you to pinch-hit. Your phone rings. It's Alex saying, "You know that meeting with Acme I'm supposed to be at? Well, I'm not going to make it. I'm stuck at the airport in Cincinnati. You'll just have to go over and make the deal for me." You ask, "But where do things stand? What am I supposed to say? What are their people like?" Alex tells you his plane is boarding and he doesn't have time to go into all that. Pinch-hitting situations, as you know, usually end with an abrupt "Just do the best you can."

What about the information other people give you about your opponents? How reliable is it? Let's say you're going to meet a group of officers from a company you want to talk merger with. You want to know as much as you can about them before actually sitting down with them face to face. You want to know the strategy they'll use, what they'll give up and what they won't. You spend some time compiling a book on them. You put into it all the information you can get from people who know the company's officers. You do the same sort of information-gathering if your objective is to get the local school board to remove an incompetent principal or to get the park district to put in a new playground.

What you learn by compiling and analyzing all the information from others is exactly what any fighter learns: much of the information you get from other people is contradictory; some is downright untrue and most of it's very doubtful. The conditions you encounter in battle are ordinarily not at all what you heard they would be. They're just different.

An effective response at such times is to move ahead and to use the action itself as the means of discovering your opponent's *suki*.

Nobunaga Oda was the first samurai general to make good tactical use of *teppo*, firearms. At times he took three thousand *teppo* specialists into battle. In the beginning of a battle he would have his *teppo* men shoot at the opponent for the sole purpose of having the opponent's riflemen return fire. From this he would calculate the number of firearms the enemy had on the battlefield. We all do a lot of rifle-counting with our opponents in business and everyday life.

In the early stages of contract negotiations in which neither side knows the other very well, each begins by making impossible demands. The demands are unimportant in themselves. Their only purpose is to help the negotiators count rifles; to get the other side to reveal what it hopes to gain.

Effective salespeople achieve their rifle-counting by observing the prospect and by listening. They're among the greatest rifle-counters and detectors of other people's *suki* in all of business. It's their job. They're always moving forward, probing, testing and trying. They're forever striking and watching what happens.

In business the best example of counting rifles is marketing. Ordinarily, when you ask people what marketing is, they say "sales." In fact, marketing and sales are not at all the same thing. When I sell you something I try to get you to buy what I have to offer. When I use the marketing approach I try to identify what will satisfy you and to supply it if I can. The only way I can find out what you want is to count your rifles.

Emery Air Freight, for one, owes its growth to dropping the sales approach and starting to count rifles. The breakthrough that changed Emery into a market-oriented rifle-counter came during negotiations with the Federal Reserve Bank of New York. Founder John Emery knew he had a valuable service to offer. So why wasn't the "Fed" buying? After long months of negotiating it suddenly came to the Emery people. The Fed wanted someone to move its bags of checks around, true; but it wanted even more someone who could devise a better system of operation. As soon as it saw what the Fed was really looking for, Emery conducted a complete study of the entire check clearance process and designed a series of services around it. From this industry Emery moved on to others—always using the rifle-counting approach.

Keep Your Eye on Your Opponent

"Expect nothing; be prepared for anything."
Samurai maxim

Some years ago Chicago Cubs third baseman Ron Santo came to the plate in the bottom of the ninth, the score tied. The first pitch came in, a perfect waist-high strike, and he belted it for a home run. Game over, Cubs win. The startled pitcher stood transfixed on the mound, able only to shout to Santo as he crossed the plate, "But you *never* go after the first pitch!" In fact, Santo "never" did, but he had this time because he had an appointment and wanted to finish the game as quickly as possible, something the pitcher was totally unaware of.

The point is: *always keep your eyes (and all of your other senses) on your opponent, not your ideas of him.* Be ready for him to jump out of your expectations and your assumptions and to do the unexpected. "Expect nothing; be prepared for anything" is a samurai motto worth remembering. Have in mind what other people have told you, but don't rely on it so heavily that you can't see what your opponent is doing right now, right in front of you. People are capable of anything at any time, no matter what you've heard about them. So be prepared for anything. In order to do this, it's necessary to see what our opponents are doing. To do that it's necessary to resist the tendency to type people.

It's been said that we no longer see people as clearly as we do after meeting them only two or three times. During the first few meetings our perceptions of them are fresher, clearer and more precise. But then, soon we form a concept of who they are and what they're like. "He's a nice guy. She's too pushy. He's sweet. She's a computer programmer. She's a Catholic. He's not very smart . . . a penny pincher . . . an easy mark," etc. In fact, we see only some of the person and a lot of our own prejudices, fears and desires.

Since the beginning of time people have tried to devise various systematic ways of classifying human types. Some have tried to pin people down on the basis of their personal traits. Then psychologist Gordon Allport took out a dictionary and found eighteen thousand words in English for different forms of behavior, many of which could coexist in a single person!

The salesman or any other human interactor who treats other people as if each were a type—an aggressive person, someone with a strong need to be liked, a pushover, etc.—completely overlooks the special aspects that make people really human—their individuality. Unfortunately, most sales training courses and books emphasize relating to prospects as if they were only types and not unique individuals at all.

The wise and effective salesman—or any human interactor-fighter—keeps his eye on the individuals he deals with and not on who he thinks they are or what "type" they've been pigeonholed into. He hits what's there, not what he thinks is there. He knows that no system of classification provides him with a fraction of the insight that *becoming the other person* (in Musashi's words) provides. He also knows that what makes people the individuals they are is their difference from other people, not their similarity.

I sent two of my salesmen to sell to an executive of one of the world's largest automobile manufacturers. One salesman was fresh out of one of those pigeonhole-the-prospect sales courses. The other had never been to a course in his life, but had a good pair of eyes. While the pigeonholer was busy trying to place the executive in the right hole, and getting nowhere, "Eyes" noticed that the executive had grease smudges on his hands and wrists. His hunch was that the executive liked to roll up his sleeves and putter around with cars—and he was right: he used that simple observation to make the sale.

Right in the middle of the meeting, Eyes suddenly blurted out, "This is an automobile company, so maybe you know someone who can help me. I've been having trouble with my car. It makes strange noises when it's idling. What do you think it could be?"

The executive pursed his lips and said, "Is it in the lot outside?"

"Yes," Eyes said.

"Let's have a look."

The three men left the office and went to the lot. Not many minutes after the executive had removed his suit jacket, thrown up the hood of Eyes' car and said "Start her up," the car was fixed and the contract had been agreed to.

"Eyes" was using *kan-ken* in action, the samurai "two eyesights." *Ken* is looking; *kan* is "seeing into," "feeling," "intuition." And the point Eyes was demonstrating was this: your opponents might be types, but they're a lot more than that—each one is an individual, and never for a moment forget it.

Techniques for Picking Up Your Opponent's Suki by Keeping All of Your Senses on Him

"See first with your mind, then with your eyes, and finally with your body."

Munenori Yagyu (1571–1646), sword master

If there is no way to learn what your opponent's *suki* is before the battle (before the sales presentation, the job interview, the party, the meeting, etc.) you have to pick it up during the action itself. Keep all your senses trained in that direction until you have a feel for that person, and then strike.

• Practice spying. "Spy" is a simple exercise you can use to develop your *suki*-spotting abilities. Spying is so much a part of spotting *suki* that the Chinese symbol for "spy" is precisely that of the Japanese *suki,* "a space between two objects."

All you have to do is simply imagine you're a spy whose job is to make accurate inferences about total strangers merely by keeping your eyes and all your other senses on them. Select any stranger—someone reading a newspaper on a train, for example, or walking toward you on the street or sitting across from you in a doctor's waiting room. Now, just by watching and listening, see how much you can figure out about that person. Keep practicing and you'll be amazed at how much you can know about people, just by observing them closely.

• Ask yourself questions about the other person. If you're using the "spy" technique with someone (while in a meeting, making a sales presentation or simply talking with a friend) and your *suki*-spotting abilities don't seem to be functioning, ask yourself these questions: Is the other person . . .

—comfortable and relaxed, or tense and nervous?
—friendly or unfriendly?
—warm, or cold and distant?
—agreeable, or disagreeable and argumentative?
—attentive or distracted?
—interested or disinterested?

• Listen, listen, listen. People are trying to tell you about themselves all the time. If you're constantly talking, how can you hear?

• Do even more than listen: in addition, look, look, look. If you do you'll be amazed how many *suki* you'll spot. It doesn't matter if you're a samurai crossing swords with an opponent or a salesman selling to a prospect, a parent talking with your children or a manager trying to get more productivity out of your staff—you have to be able to see. Memory experts estimate that 85 percent of what you remember is learned through your eyes, a fact that jibes with the term for samurai spies, "*metsuke,*" meaning "eye-attachers."

• Develop your skill at sensing intentions. The *go no sen* in karate is "counterattacking before the attack." It's responding to your opponent's intention before it becomes a physical move. You can do the very same thing—after all, you're a kind of "eye-attacher" yourself.

In practice, two *ninja* partners would stand face to face, a few feet apart. One would select a hand with which to attack. He would mentally visualize where he intended to land it on the other. The other would closely watch for any change in the attacker's appearance, any clue to when the attack would be launched and where it would be directed. The attacker would then actually launch the blow, giving the partner feedback on his hunch. After doing this repeatedly, the partner being attacked learned to know precisely, simply by close observation and *kan*, intuition, when the attack would come and where it would be targeted. He picked up the intention of his opponent. In business and social situations we can do the very same thing, since the principle guiding the *ninja*'s intention-sensing is the same as the one guiding ours: in every instance, *people have their own particular way of expressing with their body what's going on in their head.*

I have a client who I noticed grins whenever he disagrees. When he grins that way I know we're apart on that point.

Many people nod when they agree with you and glance away when they don't.

Some tense their face when they think "no" and relax it for a "yes."

Teachers have learned that a sighing student is probably a bored one, and that fast breathers are hanging on your every word. Grimaces mean gaping disagreement, and the student who gives you one of those soft, friendly, tilted-head-smiles is thinking, "He's a nice man."

All the people you know or will ever meet express what they're thinking and feeling with their bodies. That's important to know, but more important to use. Let's say you visit a new prospect or meet someone at a party for the first time and you want to get a fix on how they *show* what they're thinking. All you have to do is (1) ask them questions and (2) watch closely how they respond.

Ask something that you know will get a "yes" response. You know the prospect's name is Harry, so you say, "Your name is Harry, right?" Then just watch closely how he responds. Notice what his body does when he says "yes." *It will be doing the very same thing when he's thinking "yes" but not saying it.*

Continue your conversation and watch what he does when he says "no." Again, observe exactly what he does so that later you can pick up on his bodily responses even when he doesn't actually say "no."

Do the same with the things he will agree with and others he will disagree with, always watching his specific bodily reactions. You can follow the same procedure to judge his interest or disinterest, his liking or disliking. Noticing that his eyes get big as half-dollars when you mention the Dodgers because he's a diehard Dodger fan will help you judge his interest in other things later on.

You don't have to be with other people to sense their intentions. You can do it over the telephone by noticing changes in a person's voice volume, tempo and tone.

Some people use a fast "um-hum" when they agree and a slow "nnn" when they disagree. Once again, if you're not familiar with how certain people communicate without actually saying what's on their mind, right away ask questions with which they will agree, other questions they'll disagree with, and so on. Then just take note of the volume, pace and tone of anyone's voice and you'll be able to gauge that person's reactions.

• Imitate the other person. The body is a barometer of one's emotions. If people sit in a relaxed way they probably feel relaxed. If a man is mad as a hornet his muscles tighten, and his face has that scrunched look. Thus, a way to discover how your opponents *feel* is to imitate their bodily movements and posture. Don't be obvious about it. Just do basically what they're doing in a nonchalant way and you'll begin to feel the way they're feeling.

The samurai maxim goes: "Be as coy as a maiden until your opponent gives you an opening *(suki)*. Then be as swift as a hare and it will be too late for him to oppose you." Using the above techniques will help you to be as coy as a maiden. To be swift as a hare means using whatever *suki* you discover in your opponent whenever you attack or counterattack.

Self-knowledge: Finding the Tragic Flaw

"It's a difficult thing to truly know your own limits and points of weakness."

Hagakure, a book for samurai

The key to victory in business and personal life is to either discover or create *suki* in your opponent, and then to take advantage of it. At the same time, victory will come hard unless you prevent your opponent from uncovering *suki* in you.

In drama there's a marvelous term called "the tragic flaw." It's the tragic flaw that causes the main character's ruin, and it is always *in* the character. It's something about such characters that brings them down: their tragic flaw is the *suki* that messes them up. For example, Othello's tragic flaw was his incessant jealousy. His wife, Desdemona, wasn't really fooling around behind his back, but he was tormented by the belief that she was, and it wound up killing him.

Every individual has a tragic flaw—or two, or three—and all businesses have them. No fighter is perfect. *There is always something you do that an opponent can use against you.* You might be a person who tries to be rational and controlled. To defeat you, a wise opponent will try to drive you into an emotional state or will couch his attack in highly rational terms. Other people are easily upset. Get them mad and they can't think straight. In business many individuals act too quickly, others too slowly. Some firms are almost always Milquetoast-timid; others always choose the aggressive, toe-to-toe approach. Some people and companies are like Ken, the high school track star. You can defeat them by defeating their will.

Musashi's "You've reached the wisdom of strategy when you cannot be deceived by men" works two ways. You've reached it when you're not deceived by others and when you're not deceived by yourself. A sage once said, "Knowing others is wisdom; knowing yourself is enlightenment." In battle, this becomes: "You're skilled in defense if your opponent doesn't know what to attack."

Taking an Inventory of Your *Suki*

To discover your own *suki*, your personal tragic flaw, is a tough process of self-observation.

• Keep a book on yourself. Inventory your business and personal shortcomings and actually write them down. What do you do that brings you defeat? What is it in you that an opponent would attack?

If you refuse to put in the effort to reach your goals, that's a *suki*. Cowardice-inducing thinking too much, not taking necessary risks, self-doubt and hesitation are *suki* we looked at in Chapter 2. All inner dragons—excessive fear, worry and timidity, to name a few—are *suki*. Vanity is a *suki*. Hatred and anger are *suki*. No one is free of *suki*. What are yours? What are your company's?

• Pay close attention to your tendencies. The samurai was trained to not rely too heavily on any one strategy or striking technique, *waza*.

A *suki* itself and the source of many others in you is your own consistency. Hunters successfully stalk their prey by knowing what it can be counted on to do consistently, time after time, and the opponent who is stalking you ("you" meaning you as a person or as a company) is doing the same thing.

Right now your outer opponents are looking at your tendency to make similar types of decisions, express the same opinions, and take the same types of action most or all of the time. They know better than you that just as day follows night you can be expected to behave in a particular way under certain circumstances. If they snare you it's usually because you're predictable as hell.

We're all creatures of habit to one degree or another, but we don't have to be. We can change any habit any time we want. What are your tendencies? Your consistencies?

Make your inventory an ongoing process. Whenever you think of a personal or business *suki* of yours, jot it down. Then periodically study the list.

• Ask a friend for help. You've heard the saying, "Oh, to see ourselves as others see us." Well, why not actually do it? Involve a trusted friend in your self-assessment. My definition of a good friend is one who'll kick you in the teeth constructively. He or she levels with you to help you improve. Tell your friend, "Look, I'd really like to live my life more fully. I want to improve my business performance too. And to do that I want you to help me out." Explain the concept of *suki* and ask your friend to aid you in identifying yours.

• Eliminate your *suki*. It takes guts to look at your faults and shortcomings, even more guts to invite a friend to look at them with you, and more guts still to do something to overcome them.

Whatever *suki* your inventory has turned up, the only way to eliminate them is to act differently. If you're in the habit of preferring an A type of decision, choose B with enough regularity to keep your opponent off guard. If you "always" take a cautious, wait-and-see attitude, move boldly this time. If you're known as a procrastinator, get with it and act fast. If you avoid battles almost all the time because you fear conflict, your opponents know that's your *suki.* So they drive in at you time and again. Fight back and you destroy your *suki.* Whatever *suki* you turn up in yourself, look at it with a cold, objective eye. Then jump away from it by doing the opposite.

Points to Remember About Identifying Suki, the Gap

• Whenever you engage an opponent be aware of the strategic options available to you. Attack *(ken no sen)* works best with weak and unprepared adversaries; counterattack *(tai no sen)* avoids the vulnerability in attack strategies.

• Remember *kobo-itchi.* Literally "to swim in inconsistency," it means that the strategy you use depends on the situation; so become skilled at both attacking and counterattacking.

• *Suki o mitsukeru* is taking advantage of *suki,* a slit, crack or opening, a "space between two objects." Your opponent's *suki* is your objective whether you attack or counterattack, and whether you're a marketer, manager, salesperson, athlete or anything else. Get in the habit of looking for *suki* in everything.

• The samurai strategists were called *gunpaisha.* Their job was to keep a book on their foes. There are *gunpaisha* in all of us maintaining our books on our opponents.

• Always be prepared for your book (your *gunpai)* to be inaccurate or inadequate and to count rifles while you're in action.

• *Kan-ken,* the two eyesights of the samurai, combines observation and intuition. It's based on spotting someone else's *suki* by keeping all your senses trained on that person. *Suki*-spotting techniques in this chapter will help.

• It's difficult to know your own limits and weak points, your own personal *suki,* but it is possible. Follow the methods in this chapter and you'll be well on your way.

10

Waza:
Techniques for
Striking
Your Opponents

"It is our clan's custom to dash in, full speed, and to give the
opponent no rest."

Nobushige Takeda

Steve, a salesman, became dissatisfied with his status in the company he
worked for. He felt he should be paid more and just generally treated
better.

Symptomatic of the company's treatment—or mistreatment—of him
was the fact that he hadn't received his company-leased car yet, when
other people had gotten theirs two months earlier. Worse yet, he wasn't
getting paid as much as they were. He decided that he would go in to see
Harry, his boss, bring up the car first, then ask for a raise. Here's how
Steve described what happened.

"I'd stayed up the night before preparing for the meeting with Harry.
First thing in the morning I went in to see him. I told him right out that

I had a couple of things I wanted to talk over and he said, 'Go ahead, Steve. Shoot.' As I had planned, I'd start with the car business and move on to the real issue—my pay.

" 'Harry,' I said, 'do you realize that everyone else has their car and I haven't gotten mine yet? I'm crisscrossing the Midwest in an old heap and everyone else is tooling around in a new model, and I think it's very wrong.'

"I went on and on like that, using words like 'outrage,' 'injustice' and 'humiliating.' I mentioned my devotion to the company, my long years of service, long drives through snowstorms to keep appointments, blah-blah-blah. I brought up every kitchen sink you can imagine, constant flat tires, etc., and all the time I'm thinking, 'Man, am I setting him up. He'll be in tears any second.'

"When I ran out of breath I wound down with 'So Harry, what do you think?'

"I should never have asked! After all that, Harry says, 'The reason you haven't gotten your car yet is because we don't know if we're going to keep you, Steve!'

" 'What?'

" 'We might be letting you go. We're not sure. But if we do you won't need a company car, will you?'

"I was dumbfounded. Here I had come to ask for a raise and *better* treatment and Harry was telling me I was lucky I even had a job. I forgot all about the car—I told Harry I could make do with the old one. It wasn't too bad. So the tires were a little bald. I didn't even bring up the raise, for God's sake. I just tried to sell him on the idea of keeping me."

I was trying to work out a deal with Rick, the president of a small service company. After talking with him on the phone I went to see him. As soon as I saw him and his office I knew something was up. Here was a guy six feet eight who was wearing elevator shoes!

The guest chairs were low and cushy, almost like floor pillows. His desk, a huge, ornate, imposing mass, was elevated on a foot-high platform. What you saw when you gazed up from the visitor's chair was a man whose head looked like a turret on a brown tank.

President Lyndon Johnson was known to have advisors who had fallen out of his favor make presentations to him while he was sitting on a toilet.

Oji-waza is what Harry used on poor Steve, the striking technique of dodging or blocking, then counterattacking. Rick was trying to apply the battle principle of *debana-o-kujiki* to defeat me in the opening seconds. And LBJ was striking his advisors down by unbalancing them. That's *uchiotoshi-waza.*

Striking techniques—waza. You use them constantly, and you can bet they're constantly being used on you. Whether you're trying to sell someone on buying your product or your opinion, seeking a raise, or trying to get rid of an inner dragon that's been bringing you defeat, the principles and *waza* of striking are the same.

Striking Your Opponent's Spirit

"If the enemy stays spirited it is difficult to crush him."
Musashi Miyamoto

The samurai strike has three objects—the opponent's sword *(ken),* his technique *(waza)* and his spirit *(ki).* When you hit your opponent at the third, battle-of-spirits level, you're "penetrating the depths."

Whether you're in a meeting trying to gain a bigger budget for your division or you're out to get yourself the job, contract, promotion, terms, deal or pay you want, you're pitting your spirit against someone else's. If it's a "one against many" situation—say you're at a conference table with five, eight or ten grim-faced opponents—it's your spirit against all of theirs.

If your opponents aren't aware of the third-level, spirit-battle arena, that's their problem. But you should be, for it is at the third level that the most devastating defeats occur.

"If the enemy stays spirited it is difficult to crush him," says Musashi. Even if you're not out to crush the other guy, but simply to get more of what you want, drive in at his spirit. Here are some tips that will help.

• Control your thoughts. A sixteenth-century samurai general assembled his troops and told them, "The essential thing is the mind." The road to the spirit—yours and your opponent's—is through the mind. All victories are first won there, and all losses first occur there too. It has nothing to do with IQ, but with *nei-kung,* inner power.

Winners make positive assumptions about success—they are confident of winning. Losers expect defeat. Kendo master Jirokichi Yamada's "It's before the match that who wins and loses is decided" is true of any match—in the *dojo*, boardroom or kitchen.

Controlling how you think is the guiding principle of battles of the spirit. "Go to the battle firmly confident of victory," says sixteenth-century samurai general Kenshin Uesugi, "and you will return home with no wounds whatsoever." So—whenever you're going up against any opponent—*Think confidently, think you'll win.*

If you're about to ask for a raise and thinking, "There's no way I'll get it. This meeting shouldn't take long," *stop* and replace those thoughts with confident thoughts. Do that time and again and you will already be nearer to victory, and your opponent closer to defeat.

• Increase your *ki.* Recall what was said in Chapter 4: *ki* is energy, a frame of mind and a force you generate which affects other people. To *ki o mitasu,* or "fill yourself with *ki*"—

• Make sure your mind holds only positive thoughts and intentionally rejects all negatives. Remember, you possess the ability to direct your attention any way you wish to, wherever you wish to. Direct it toward victory time and again and your chances of winning will increase accordingly.

• Focus on your one point two inches below your navel.

• Launch into your deep abdominal diaphragmatic breathing.

When your *ki* is lively and buoyant your actions are confident and sure. You *feel* it and your opponent *sees* it and *feels* it coming from you.

• Create a block to action in your opponent. Samurai *unnerving techniques* are designed to create *suki* in your opponent. Remember the blocks to action we saw in chapter two—fear of taking chances, thinking too much, self-doubt and hesitation? Create any of these blocks in your opponents and they will open a *suki* for you.

Unnerving Technique One: Control Your Opponent's Expectations

If you're a wise warrior, your battles with your opponents start before their battles with you. Joe Girard makes no secret of the fact that he is the greatest salesman in the world, or that he is listed as such in the *Guinness Book of World Records.* He advertises his well-deserved title, and when prospects come to him they *expect* to be sold. They place their spirit right into his able hands. He's applying the samurai principle of "win first, fight later."

You can bet that one reason Musashi won so often was that his reputation preceded him. Here was a man who was so confident of victory that he actually napped before the biggest fight of his life. Word gets around about that kind of confidence.

Athletes are wonderful unnervers. Off the field, Hall of Fame middle linebacker Dick Butkus is a mild, soft-spoken and sensitive man. On it, he was a terrifying presence who purposely fed his reputation as "Mr. Mean." He once reported to a roomful of newspapermen that he had a recurring dream in which he tackled a running back so hard that he knocked his head off. Imagine yourself a little running back reading *that* in the paper. Did Butkus actually have the dream? Who cares? All that mattered was that the opponent *believed* he did and that Butkus had his spirit before the game even began.

Unnerving Technique Two: *Kyojitsu Ten Kan Ho,* Presenting Falsehood as Truth

"All warfare," wrote Sonshi, "is based on deception. If you're able to attack, seem unable. When using your forces, appear inactive. When you're near, make him think you're far away."

Musashi used to come in strong, then move his feet more quickly than the opponent expected, distracting the enemy—a kind of Ali shuffle. The business equivalent of this move is to do something, anything, that distracts your opponents and makes your attack surprising. Feint a cut and let them handle it, then come in with your real blow. Make them think you want one thing when you really want something else. Lead them to believe that you're going to market product X in the Midwest when you're really planning to push product Y along the East Coast. Get their attention off the real thing and onto the phony thing.

I had accompanied Jerry to a meeting to discuss a contract between his medium-sized company and a very large, multi-billion-dollar firm. Representing the big company were three highly skilled negotiators.

Through the afternoon the list of issues was discussed. Each was settled amicably until only two remained: one, which company would maintain control over day-to-day matters related to the joint effort; and two, the percentage of the profits Jerry's company would receive.

With the first of these issues, things bogged down. Jerry opened by saying, "Since we developed the concept and did all the backup research it's really more our baby than yours. We demand control over it to see that it's done right. That's our position and nothing you can say or do will make us change our minds."

Even as he was talking it was obvious that the three men on the other side of the table were provoked. For it had become clear to me that these men and their company wanted, needed to feel they were in control of things. For Jerry to be so adamant was tantamount to saying there wouldn't be a deal after all.

The control issue was charged with emotion for the three and the meeting got hot. For hours they went around on that one issue: what Jerry wanted wasn't logical, wasn't practical; their company had never let go of control.

Through the windows of the meeting room I watched the sun set, and still the hassle continued. Finally, one of the three shouted, "Since when does the minnow (Jerry's little company) tell the whale (their *big* firm) what to do?"

With that, normally easygoing Jerry jumped up, pounded his fist on the conference table and yelled, "That's it, damn it. That's it. I've had enough of this b.s." He kicked the chair out of his way, gathered his papers and stormed out of the room.

Shocked, the three stared at each other momentarily, then went out after Jerry and brought him back in.

"Jerry," one said, "you know we want to work with you. There's plenty of money to be made by all. But look at it from our point of view. There's nothing we can do. Our hands are tied. There is just no precedent for what you're proposing."

Jerry took a deep breath. Quietly, as if beaten, he said, "O.K., you win. You got the better of me. You hammered me down. But you owe me."

With peace restored, one of the three said, "All that's left is the last issue. Jerry's people want 50 percent."

Quickly, Jerry said, "You whipped me on the control issue. Surely you're not going to start up on the split."

There was a crucial pause. "O.K.," said the senior of the three.

On the way to the plane to take us home I said to Jerry, "All you were really after was the 50 percent."

He smiled. "Right. We don't even *want* control. But I had to get their attention off the 50 percent split and onto something else. Since I knew their 'thing' was control, I made that the fight, not the money."

Shingen Takeda (1521–73) and Kenshin Uesugi (1530–78) were arch-rivals and neighbors who engaged each other in battle on five occasions between 1553 and 1564. Both were known for their tactics of trickery and deception. Yet, when Kenshin learned that Shingen's troops and civilians were without salt because the lords supplying Shingen had turned against him, Kenshin generously supplied his enemy with all the salt he required. It was outrageous, Kenshin said, that fighting be conducted anywhere but on the battlefield. On the battlefield, however, the inevitability of the situation dictates that the fighter use his full reper-toire of skills, including deception.

If you personally find deception morally repugnant, forget I ever men-tioned *kyojitsu ten kan ho.* But if you don't, there are many ways you can use it to gain control of your opponent's spirit.

Unnerving Technique Three: Present the *Yugamae* (Bow-Holding Posture) You Wish Your Opponent to See

The samurai is taught, "Frighten your opponent with your body." Look like someone to be reckoned with and you already are.

Your body. If you're in good physical shape you're the exception. Most men and women in sedentary jobs are in miserable condition and look terrible. Spindly legs and fat, soft bellies inspire respect in no one. If you don't have time to go to a gym or health club, don't. Do the following to develop your—

Calves: Stand on your feet and rise on your toes;

Thighs: Do deep knee bends;

Stomach: Do sit-ups; lie on your back and lift your legs until they are over your navel, then lower and repeat;

Buttocks: Kneel and place your hands on the floor in front of you, holding your arms rigid; then thrust one leg at a time to your rear high overhead.

Arms, chest, shoulders, neck, back: Get a book on simple weight-lifting exercises, barbells and some weights, and lift, lift, lift.

Your clothes. The *ninja* were the most ingenious of all Eastern fighters. One device they used was the disguise. They slipped under their enemies' noses dressed as monks, beggars, farmers and women. You and I know that disguises are a part of modern business and social life too.

There are really no "right" clothes or "wrong" clothes *per se*. Getting the other person to think, "Wow, this guy's wearing a thousand-dollar suit," may be effective at times, but at other times can backfire: "Rich city slicker." The right clothes for battle are the ones that help you gain control of your opponent's spirit by creating an impression of you that contributes to your victory.

Luggage. If you work in the business world, your attaché case is as much a part of your fighting uniform as the sword was a part of the samurai's. Where you go, it goes. You lug (gage) around your image in it. Use it, too, to help create the impression you want your opponent to have of you.

Before going into battle, decide on the impression you're trying to create in your opponent's mind. Then appear the way you need to.

Keeping Your Opponent from Striking Your Spirit

"A warrior must only take care that his spirit is never broken."
                                                        Shissai

Ted Turner is one of the greatest success stories of American business in recent years. He owns a television network, the Atlanta Braves baseball team and basketball's Atlanta Hawks, among other enterprises. His time is estimated to be worth twenty thousand dollars an hour. None of these ventures came easily to Turner. He created them, often against high odds and the advice of experts. He fought for everything he has.

For all his money, Turner refuses to buy a private jet (which he could easily afford), flies coach, not first class, hasn't had a shoeshine in fifteen years, wears inexpensive clothes and cuts his own hair.

The point of mentioning Ted Turner is not to suggest that you will become rich if you start staying away from barbershops and clothing stores. The point is, no outer weapon or resource ever makes a fighter—not a sword, a fine suit, an elegant calfskin briefcase; and not fame, shined shoes, riches or status. Your most effective fighting weapons are always inside you—your attitudes, spirit, will, energy, power, knowledge of strategies and strikes and your driving commitment to move forward, always forward.

At the same time you're after your opponents' spirit, if they are skilled they're after yours. Never let them get it.

They've got it as soon as you walk into someone's office and think: "God, just look at this beautiful place. It cost more to furnish this office than my entire house. What am I doing here anyway?" Or,

"He's got a *Who's Who in America* on his desk, and it's opened *to his name.* As for me, well, I'm just little old me."

The samurai always tries to gain slightly higher ground than his adversary. Whatever you do, strive to keep your opponent from getting higher than you in any way, physically or figuratively.

Higher ground in the literal sense is what Rick, the six-foot-eight elevator-shoe-wearer, was trying to gain on me. The message of his classic look-down-on-your-opponent arrangement was: "I'm way up here. I'm superior. You're way down there. You're subordinate."

After sitting in the cushy chair for three seconds I went out to the waiting room, found a tall, straight-back chair, placed it *on* the platform next to Rick's desk and then began the meeting.

There are three main techniques for countering your opponent's attempts to reach higher ground figuratively. The *put-down* can be very deflating. If people are trying to impress you with their wealth by flashing a lot of jewelry, for example, the put-down response would be to comment on how you prefer not to wear anything like that because it's too gaudy and in bad taste.

One mental put-down that's commonly used is imagining your opponent sitting in front of you in his undershorts. It's very difficult to be unnerved by a man doing battle in his Jockeys.

Far more effective than the put-down is simply *refusing to be impressed* by your opponents or anything about them. The samurai believes that you gain the strength of two men merely by refusing to retreat from something. Replace awe of anyone with a so-what attitude and you put a stop to all kinds of mental retreat. If a man has a large, beautifully furnished office, so what? If he is wearing expensive, hand-tailored clothes and flashy jewelry, so what? A fat bank account—so what?

Asked which type of spear was the best to use in battle, Shissai laughed and replied, "The spear with which one thrusts." In other words, the *person*, not the weapon, is the important thing in all your battles.

Your business competitors might be sitting in plush offices with rows of computers wheezing and whirling all around, with an army of staff at their disposal. And your office might be a room in your home that you share with a mangy dog and two parakeets. So what? They've got you with outer weaponry, but if they don't have a spirit that can knock down a wall, and you do, I'll put my money on you.

The third technique for countering your opponents' attempts to reach higher ground is to *move forward zan-totsu,* "closing and striking." Keep moving forward to where you want to be and it will be very hard for anyone or anything to break your spirit.

Timing and the Right Time

"Don't always think in a straight line."
The Way of the Spear

In business development, success often follows a product whose time has come: B. F. Goodrich introduced the rubber tires needed by the growing automobile industry; Hertz Rent A Car prospered after World War II when consumers wanted mobility without necessarily owning a car; Glidden invented barbed wire when the West was being tamed; the Gillette safety razor appeared at precisely the time the beard was going out of fashion.

In *every* battle there are opportune moments for you to strike. The art of timing is recognizing when the opportune moment is upon you and taking advantage of it immediately.

The opportune moment is when you spot *suki,* the gap. Whenever you see it, strike. Drive in and hit before your opponent has a chance to recover. This is the skill of *katsujin no ken,* or "taking advantage of your opponent's moves." While *suki* may appear at any time, there are three points when it is most likely to appear:

1. As your opponents prepare to make their move;
2. Right after they have completed a move; or
3. When they are relaxed without being ready.

1. Hitting Your Opponents as They Prepare to Make Their Move

Debana-waza. The *shikake-waza* (offensive) technique of attacking at the start.

When your opponents start their move they are vulnerable to your strike. Why? Because they have not yet concentrated their mind or strength fully. They are getting there, but they're not there yet. They are like small waves that will pick up strength, rising to huge, powerful breakers. Hit while your opponent is still a small wave. Dash forward *mo chih ch'u,* without hesitation. This is "deploying your troops after the enemy but arriving before he does."

I can illustrate *debana-waza,* attacking-at-the-start striking, through something that happened to a good friend of mine. Mary came up with an original method for selling children's books to schools and the general public. After explaining it to me, she said she thought maybe she would start small and build the business slowly. Then she asked in a sheepish, maybe-it's-not-a-very-good-idea-after-all voice, "What do you think?"

What did I think? It was absolutely beautiful—an incredibly ingenious idea. All the great entrepreneurs of the past were smiling in their graves.

It was such a marvelous idea, and held promise of leading to so much income, that Mary didn't stand a chance if she started small. "Start small and that's as big as you'll ever get," I said. "Some powerful competitor will see what a great idea it is and will pump money into it, putting you out of business completely."

Some people seem temperamentally unsuited to comprehending the tough realities of *debana-waza,* and Mary was one of them. "You don't understand," she said. "No one runs a business like this. There is no competition." And I said, "There will be." I suggested that she start right out in a "big wave" fashion, getting as much capital as she could from investors. But she didn't. She started small and slow, and sure enough the competitor did appear—a large corporation. It analyzed what little Mary was doing, invested hundreds of thousands of dollars into doing it bigger, better and faster, and stole Mary's market right from under her. It wasn't long before Mary lost her business and went deeply into debt.

There are many adversaries that it's best to hit *debana-waza,* right at the start. Your inner opponents, for example:

• Fall off a horse and don't get right back up on it and you'll have a tough time defeating your fear of falling. But climb back up into the saddle right away in *debana-waza* fashion and you're riding again before the fear tells you you can't.

• Any kind of emotional disturbance—fear, worry, nervousness, anxiety and depression—is best defeated as it's beginning its move against you. If you wait until it's a big wave you might have to swim for your life. Better to strike *debana-waza,* when it's still just a little ripple of feeling.

• Harmful habits, too, are ripe for striking right away. From overeating to drinking or gambling too much, they are best defeated with *debana-waza.* Hit them while they're still just tendencies.

"You mean to tell me that the reason you've refused to speak to me for the last thirteen years is *that?* For heaven's sake why didn't you just say something?" If anything like that ever happened to you, you already know how important *debana-waza* is in resolving conflicts and differences of opinion.

The opportune moment to settle differences is when they're still small waves. Let time pass and they have a habit of becoming tidal waves of "I used to dislike you; now I can't stand you" hostility.

In virtually every disagreement there is a *core of mutual agreement,* something both sides can agree to, however small and obscure it might be at first. If you can cut through your differences, find that core of agreement and build on it you can avoid any number of fights.

• Husbands and wives often find themselves arguing, sometimes bitterly, about how to raise their children. One parent says X is better and the other says Y. If each would just stop to use *debana-waza*, it wouldn't be long before both came to recognize their core of mutual agreement—that they both want the very best for their children.

• Business associates, too, get sucked into nasty and needless fights. If they were to drop their combat attitude and right away, *debana-waza*, find the core of agreement, they would not fight each other, but the competition.

• Salesmen often find themselves at loggerheads with a prospect. Buyers only want what's best for themselves or their firm. The successful salesmen are the ones who are able to demonstrate with *debana-waza* quickness that they want *exactly* the same things for the prospect.

2. Hitting Them Right After They Have Made a Move

Oji-waza. The technique of dodging or blocking, then counterattacking.

A second opportune moment comes when your opponents have committed themselves completely to a move and you've dodged it. Now they find themselves strung out in a motion that didn't work. In that moment they are vulnerable. They have revealed a gap, a *suki*. If you go in right then and there with all your power, you've got a good chance to nail them with a devastating strike. Musashi calls this treading down your opponent's sword to prevent him from rising to the attack a second time. Tread and stomp with everything you have—your abilities, spirit and weapons.

Remember Steve, the fellow who went in to ask Harry for a new car and a raise? Well, Steve got treaded on. Musashi had nothing on old Harry. He let Steve make his attack move, then met it with a powerful and, to say the least, devastating counterattack. That's *oji-waza*.

If you're a person who hits your opponents right after they have made their move you're an *oji-waza* user. It can be extremely effective, as you have no doubt discovered. But there is a drawback. Perhaps you've learned what it is. For *oji-waza* to work, *your opponents have got to attack,* and sometimes they won't.

Samurai sword fights would sometimes last two or three hours or longer, with neither man making any move at all. Each was waiting for the other to attack and neither did. Many business meetings are like that —no winners but a lot of draws.

You're a good counterattacker, but your opponent won't attack. What do you do? You might try using . . .

. . . Ittosai's Playing-Possum Technique

Ittosai was a master of the sword who based his "cutting down" school not on physical skill but on the psychology of opponents: *Know how your opponents think and you'll know their intentions.* Know their intentions *and they're under your control.*

"What do all outer opponents have in common?" asked Ittosai. His answer: the urge to win. Given this, he reasoned that the way to defeat them was to exploit their urge by playing possum. If you're a good counterattacker and your opponent won't attack, take the Ittosai approach. Pretend a *suki.* Make believe you're weak or unprepared so your opponent will come after you.

One Chinese Kung Fu technique is called "the drunken style." The drunken-style fighter actually pretends he is drunk, staggering around and reeling as if intoxicated. Watching such a helpless person falling over himself, the opponent becomes overconfident. Imagine his surprise when suddenly the drunk lands a perfect kick to his head!

When you employ the Ittosai playing-possum approach you're using your opponents' thought processes as weapons against them. You're planting ideas in their mind one by one, and when your opponent adds them up they equal "Hmm, I can beat this person."

It's the exact opposite of *un-*nerving. It's *en-*couraging. It's purposely providing the other person with the courage to move against you.

You do it by suggesting or stating something that will make your opponent think: "This guy's bargaining position is weak." Or, "He's weak, he doesn't have any guts." "Sounds confused and unsure of himself." "I can take advantage of his impatience." "He's vacillating."

. . . or *look* the way that will get him to think, "I can take this poor guy." Many a businessman has worn a second- or a third-best suit to a meeting for the sole purpose of creating an image of inferiority. And a great many salespeople purposely make themselves appear awkward and non-assertive, even timid, in order to encourage the prospect to try taking advantage of them.

3. Striking when Your Opponent Is Relaxed and Not Ready

Uchiotoshi-waza. The technique of striking down your opponent's sword when he is out of balance.

The third right moment for your strike comes when your opponent is relaxed. There is strength in relaxation if it's coupled with poise and readiness for action. But this type of opportune moment for *uchiotoshi-waza* appears when your adversary is too relaxed.

Chuck, a marketing specialist, was not effective in winning over others to his view in meetings. His arguments were sound and well thought-out and he was articulate enough, so what was the problem?

We talked it over and decided that the flaw in his style was bad timing and that *uchiotoshi* held the solution. He had been attempting to make his point when the resistance of others in the meetings was high, coming in with his big point first, rather than advancing when the others' opposition was lower.

He applied *uchiotoshi-waza*, striking when the others were out of balance: before every meeting he would identify the one particularly persuasive point—such as the most dramatic statistic, potent demonstration or powerful example—that would support his position. Holding this in reserve during the meeting, he would offer his subpoints, which others in the meeting would usually counter one after another.

Then, the moment he saw the others relax their guard, believing they had beaten him back point by point and assuming that the meeting was just about over, Chuck would come in with his persuasive zinger: not in a hard, tough, argumentative manner that would, he discovered, quickly rekindle resistance, but in a casual, easygoing fashion . . . "Incidentally, our research shows that two of our leading competitors have used precisely the same strategy and it's made them eleven million dollars overnight."

A fighter can often defeat a superior opponent in a grueling fight if he can outlast him. Even if you are fighting against others who are better fighters than you are, you will always have an edge on them if you can exhaust them by forcing them to try to keep up with you. If you never give up and never let them give up you can win through sheer endurance.

Skillful salesmen make a fair share of their sales immediately after the prospect has piled on one objection after another and even heaped some personal abuse on them to boot. An onlooker might think, "No way this guy will make a sale." But if the salesman waits patiently, allowing the now hot-under-the-collar prospect to ventilate, eventually the buyer will quiet down. Right at that point, when the tirade is over, the skillful salesman will make his *uchiotoshi-waza* move, asking for the order. Try it yourself. It can lead to sales.

It's quite possible to *induce relaxation suki* in your opponent by pretending to be relaxed yourself. This is called "to pass on." Pass on or transmit your spirit of relaxation to your adversary, then sweep in powerfully, your mind sharp, fully committed to the attack.

A group of samurai were playing *Go* one night. Master Kitabatake* was sitting on the side watching the game. When he made a suggestion, one of the men pulled out a sword and wounded him slightly. The others jumped up and subdued the attacker.

"It's my own fault and I apologize," Kitabatake said. "No harm done. I'm sorry."

When the attacker had calmed down and approached Kitabatake with a cup of *sake*, Kitabatake drew his sword and cut him down with one blow.

You've probably noticed that in basketball when one side becomes sloppy this tendency is passed on to the other team and they both get sloppy. It also happens in business. You can make it work for you by pretending to play sloppily while keeping your mind sharp and focused and taking advantage of your opponent's relaxation *suki*.

Let's say you have been hard at it in a meeting. You and your adversary have been putting everything into it, parrying and feinting, but to no avail. If you then act bored or give off a disinterested I-couldn't-careless attitude, or simply relax in your chair and change the subject, it will lower your opponent's concentration and perhaps make him careless.

Coming at your opponent from an *unexpected direction* is another way

---

* The Kitabatake were an influential warrior clan from the central province of Ise.

to induce relaxation *suki.* Musashi applied this principle in his development of an unorthodox style of lateral movement.

Jerry, the fellow whom we saw in this chapter negotiating a deal with a large corporation, applied the same principle. He induced relaxation over how the profits would be shared (the *real* issue for him) by coming in at an unexpected point—the control issue.

More Tips on Striking

"Stick to the larger view of things. If your vision is narrow, your spirit will be narrow."

Bukko

- *Strike what's there, not what isn't.*

Chris headed a medium-sized organization. He was one of the most brilliant people I've ever met. And he was energetic, courageous, charismatic and knowledgeable. His one *suki,* his one gaping flaw, was his inability to do anything simply.

Actions that really needed only one or two easy swipes of his managerial sword he complicated into a mile-long string of tedious and complicated approaches and stages of implementation which first confused, then alienated his work force. Suddenly there were union problems, morale problems and productivity problems—all of his creation and none of which should ever have arisen. Unfortunately they remained years after he had been fired.

If we're not careful we can easily become much too clever, in business management and in our life management too. I know very well that right now you can name at least a handful of very bright people who can recite all kinds of complicated reasons why they don't make more of themselves, or lose that weight they're always complaining about, or solve their other problems.

The samurai wasn't nearly as clever. Tell him that you have analyzed the situation and decided that the reason you have a weight problem is that you were spoiled as a child, or have an unconscious desire to be fat so people will reject you, or you suffer from a chronic inferiority complex etc., etc., etc., and he will grimace a little.

Wherever you find them, all warriors hold the samurai value of *wabi*, simplicity, unpretentiousness and naturalness. When all is said and done, all that matters is that your opponents are right there, right in front of you. So strike them, cleanly and directly. That's it.

Whenever you face a problem, tough situation, emotional block, crisis or any other opponent, try the *wabi* approach. Ask yourself, "When I drop all the complications that my fertile brain is creating—when I slice this thing down to its barest bones—what's left, right now, right in front of me?" That's your opponent.

Then ask, "Now what is the most simple and direct way to beat it?" Have the good sense to be as stupid as a samurai. Then strike.

• *When the advantage swings to you, chase.*

In all battles—from battle-of-the-bulge dieting to battles in the marketplace or driving to your big life goals—there is a particular moment when the advantage swings to one side or the other. Whenever the advantage swings to your side in any area of life, immediately concentrate your attack more forcefully. Use the "chasing attack." Strike so that your opponents don't have a chance to recover. When you see them losing ground and their spirit sagging, redouble your effort. If you're in a meeting, sit up straight, be alert and energetic and advance on your opponent. If your product's sales finally inch past your competitors', don't waste your energy patting yourself on the back. Say, instead, "We've got them on the run. How do we get them to run faster?" If you spot your opponents' morale declining, figure out a way to hit harder so that it will plunge faster and lower.

• *When the advantage swings away from you, get it back.*

The most decisive losses to the losing side happen when it is in retreat. Inner opponent or outer, it makes no difference; having gotten the advantage away from you, your adversary will usually chase you and pick you off.

The advantage is like a ball passing between you and your opponents. Sometimes you have it; sometimes they have it. Don't delude yourself into believing you've got it when they do. When you see them with it, don't panic; just coolly realize they're holding it. You don't have to have the ball all the time during the fight; just make sure you have it when the battle ends.

In meetings of any kind, when someone else holds the advantage and you find it difficult to get it back it often makes sense to call for a break in the action as a defensive move. Musashi call this *yotsu te o hanasu*, "to release four hands." Better to regroup and rejuvenate your spirit than to allow the other person to use the chasing attack against you.

I once combined calling for a *yotsu te o hanasu* break in the action with gathering additional information—unintentionally. I was trying to sell a new service to executives of a large manufacturer. The meeting had been dragging on for about four hours. Sometimes they had the advantage ball and sometimes I had it, but they had had it for a damned long time, and I could not get it back. So I said I had to use the washroom.

I left the conference room and started down the corridor to think things over. Suddenly I had a hunch I should go back. What I found made me very happy.

A lot of smoking had been going on during the meeting, and to air out the room while I was gone they had left the door open. They were talking over the compromises they were willing to make to strike an agreement with me. All I had to do was stand outside the door and listen. I felt an awful lot like a *ninja*. When they were done, I went to the washroom, freshened up and figured out what my approach would be, then returned to the meeting and got the advantage right back.

The swing of the advantage occurs in the course of everyday events too. The advantage swing is in everything and every aspect of life. No matter how much samurai operating you do, for periods of time one success after another will come your way, then you'll be thrown for a loss.

Be ready for the swing of the advantage away from you. Realize that it's happening. Be able to say, "Oops, there goes the swing of the advantage." Then use your skill as a fighter to get it back.

• *Stick to your opponents like glue.*

Let no gap open between you and your opponents—ever. Stick to them like glue whether they are people or problems. Stay right with them. Don't let them get away. Wherever they go, you go. When they retreat, advance. If they dash away, go after them.

Sticking to your opponent like glue applies to everything you battle.

• Remember Smirnoff's Eli Shapiro, the salesman whose perseverance made Smirnoff? When he waited those long tedious hours in prospects' offices day after day he was sticking like glue.

• If you're trying to make a better life for yourself and your family there are scores of blocks that stand in your way. To whittle them down one by one you've got to stick to each and every one of them until you've knocked them off.

• If your competitors are beating the stuffings out of you time and again and you want to defeat them, stick to them like glue.

• Glue-sticking in job-hunting means realizing that it isn't enough merely to submit a resumé. Follow up, call, write thank-you-for-the-interview letters, let people know you want the job.

• High sales producers simply ask for the order more frequently than low producers. Just asking people very directly for whatever you want from them is great glue-sticking. Sales rise between 20 and 40 percent when salespeople make it a point just to ask for the order. Ask for what you want in your life and your sales will rise too.

• Marketing glue-sticking means staying with your consumers wherever they go. To induce a straight-razor-using public to buy his new safety razor, King Gillette gave the razor away free, having decided, rightly, that (1) what consumers want is something for nothing, and (2) his real business was not razors anyway, but blades.

• Glue-sticking in meetings means refusing to be lured off the subject you want to talk about. To stick like glue, always, at every moment, know precisely what you want the meeting to focus on; where it is at any point in time; when someone is moving it off the subject; how to nudge it back.

• To defeat your inner opponents and strike through the dragon's mask you have to stick like glue.

If shyness is an inner opponent, as it is for many people, don't say, "Oh well, that's the way I am." If you're unhappy about shyness do something about it. No one *has* to be any particular way, including shy. You can overcome anything if you stick to it with everything you've got.

• Glue-sticking also means finding ways to cut down the distance between yourself and your goals. Many people fail to reach their goals simply because they let too much distance open up. On the other hand, successful people invariably find ways of overcoming obstacles. They go through, under, over or around them, but they find a way. They're always pressing and moving, always closing ground, always going in. Constantly remind yourself of what your goals really are; then stick to them like superglue.

• *Beware of a desperate foe.*

Having surrounded the enemy's city, a general sent a stern written message to the defenders saying, "You will all be buried. Not a single life will be spared."

Every attack the general launched was met with stiff resistance, and each time his warriors fell back. "They are well supplied with food and fight with blind fury," the general was told by his troops. Days and weeks passed and the result was always the same. The surrounded garrison fought relentlessly. With the casualty count running high and realizing that no matter what he did he could not win, the general withdrew his troops.

There are many such tales in the samurai Way, all illustrating that if you leave your opponents no alternative to dying, they will fight you to the death—and it may be yours.

Leave a company or an individual no recourse but to sign a devastatingly unfair contract and—although the contract will be signed—*you* will come to rue the day. If you're a manager and you shaft your workers you will come to rue that day too. "Output restriction"—workers purposely holding back on their productivity—is just an academic nicety for *kataki-uchi,* samurai revenge, vendetta. People who fast-talk their way to the sale of a clinker are fair game for *kataki-uchi.*

Revenge is one of the most powerful motives in many people, particularly in business. They are the Rocky Balboas of the world. No matter how hard you hit them, they won't stay down. So,

> Don't make your foes desperate. If they're already
> desperate, don't press them too hard.

Shaft, gyp, humiliate or demean your opponents, particularly if they're the Rocky or samurai kind, and you'll have to learn to sleep with your eyes open. Even then don't bet on having to do it too long.

Waza Applications

"Always strike somewhere."
Samurai maxim

• Start with this point: you will win no victory without attacking, *shikake-waza* style, or counterattacking, *oji-waza.* If you're trying to lose weight or bad habits, or improve your career situation, *you must pick up your sword and strike.*

• Survey your life, looking for the opportunities you had to strike, in and out of business, and didn't take advantage of. Think of all the chances that were wide open to you but you did nothing about.

• Now vow never to let that happen again. Commit yourself to striking whenever the *suki* of opportunity opens to you. Promise yourself that from this point on you're going to wedge yourself into every *suki,* every gap, each opening wherever you see it appear.

• Acquire the habit of seeing situations in your life in terms of *waza.* Don't leave this book's information on these pages; take it and *do* something with it. Make *waza* a part of your everyday thought process and vocabulary. For example, be able to say, "What just happened to me was pure *oji-waza* counterattack," or, "I've got to *debana-waza* my way out of this problem."

• Pay particular attention to taking care that your spirit is never broken. "The mind is the essential thing." Your mind. Keep it filled with expectations of victory no matter what. Ten times a day—a hundred times—shake all thoughts of defeat from your head and learn to expect to win.

• Develop your skills using not just one or two, but each of the *waza.* The principle of striking is the same in private life as in corporate life: always mix your moves.

• Don't complicate your battles. Choose the *wabi* course—simplify. Boil your battles down to their purest essence, then strike what's there.

• Begin to see life as swings of the advantage, *to* you at times and at other times *away* from you. When the advantage in anything comes to you, always advance, chasing your opponent. When it swings away from you, calmly and coolly realize what's happened, then retrieve it.

• There's a moral law in fighting, and it's this: "For whatsoever a man soweth, that shall he also reap." Whatever you do, don't drive an opponent to *kataki-uchi* vendetta or revenge against you. Never make a foe desperate.

• Last, *always stick to your opponents like glue.* That applies to every battle. Never let gaps open between you and what you want. Always close ground.

A Final Thought

When a samurai battle had ended and all had grown quiet, you might suddenly hear the famous cry, *Katte, kabuto no o o shime yo!* "After victory, tighten your helmet cords!"

You have applied the skills of the samurai and won the battle of the moment. Now tighten your helmet cords and get ready for the next.

Glossary

ai	Harmony, accord.
aikido	Japanese unarmed martial art; literally, the Way *(do)* of harmonizing *(ai)* with your opponent's spirit *(ki)*.
akirame	Resignation.
arasoi	Strife.
ashigaru	Foot soldier.
bado	Horsemanship.
bakufu	Samurai government under a shogun.
bodo	The Way of the staff.
budo	The Way of life of the samurai warrior.
buke	Warrior families.
bunbu ryodo	The united Ways of the pen and the sword.
bushi	Elite samurai.
bushi no toryo	Warrior chieftain.
bushido	The samurai code of conduct.
chado	The Way of tea.
chi	Chinese equivalent of Japanese *ki*.
chikara	Physical strength.
Chushingura	Story of the forty-seven *ronin*.
daido	A principle that operates in all things; life principle.
daimyo	Lord.
daisho	Two swords worn by the samurai, one long and one short.
debana-o-kujiki	To defeat in opening seconds.
debana-waza	Attacking at the start.
do	Way.
dojo	Training hall; literally, Way *(do)* place *(jo)*.
fudoshin	Immovable mind.
gen	Illusion.
gi	Technique.
giri	Duty.
Go	A popular Japanese board game.

gunpai	Large metal fans carried into battle on which was inscribed information pertinent to the conduct of the battle.
gunpaisha	Keepers of *gunpai*, strategists.
hakarai	Suppression.
hara-kiri	Honorable death of suicide; also called *seppuku*.
iaido	Sword-drawing.
iaidoka	Practitioner of *iaido*.
isagi-yoku	The art of dying well; being fully prepared to die.
isshin	One mind; singlemindedness.
iwao no mi	"Rock body."
jodo	The Way of the stick.
joriki	The power of concentration.
ju	Flexible adaptation.
judo	Hand-to-hand martial art based on flexible adaptation.
juttedo	The Way of the truncheon.
ka	Suffix meaning practitioner of, as in *aikidoka*.
kakuto bugei	Fighting techniques.
kamae	Battle stance; posture.
kan	Intuition.
kan-ken	Two eyesights. *Ken* is "looking," *kan* is "seeing into," or intuition.
karate	Unarmed martial art originating in Okinawa; literally, "empty" *(kara)* "hand" *(te)*. There are wide differences among the more than seventy types of Japanese *karate*, but all involve sparring and grappling techniques and *atemi*, blows delivered to vulnerable parts of the body.
kataki-uchi	Revenge, vendetta.
katana	Long sword.
katchu	Battle armor.
katsujin no ken	Samurai striking art of taking advantage of an opponent's moves.
katzu	Battle shout.
ken	Sword.
ken no sen	Strategy of attack.
ken no shinzui	Real goal of swordsmanship.
kendo	Swordsmanship; the Way of the sword.
kengo	Expert swordsman.
ki	Energy; spirit; aura; vitality; breath; life force; inner strength.

ki ken tai no ichi	"The complete unity of the mind, heart and body with the sword."
Ki o mitasu	"Fill yourself with *ki*."
kobo-itchi	Principle that choice of strategy depends on the situation.
koiguchi	Open slot of the scabbard.
kotsunen nenki	A sudden illumination.
kufu	Struggling, wrestling and grappling with something until a way out is found.
Kung Fu	Literally meaning mastery; commonly used as a general term for all Chinese martial arts.
kyojitsu ten kan ho	Presenting falsehood as truth; deception.
kyudo	Archery; the Way of the bow.
makoto	Sincerity; putting *everything* into an act, without reservation.
marui	Circular motion.
meijin	Master of a Way.
metsuke	"Eye attachers"; spies.
Minamoto	Family of warriors; enemies of the Taira.
misai no ichinen	Trace of thought.
Mokuteki hon'i	"Focus on your purpose."
mo chih ch'u	Acting (going ahead) without hesitation.
musha-shugyo	Training in warriorship.
mushin	No-mindedness; without thought.
naginatado	Halberd fighting.
naiki	Doctrine of *ki.*
nei-kung	Inner power (Chinese term).
nukazu ni sumu	Settling disputes "without pulling out the sword."
oji-waza	"Receiving techniques"; counterattack strategy.
ronin	Samurai no longer in the employ of a master; literally, "wave men."
ryoku	Physical power.
ryu	School of a martial Way.
samurai	Warrior.
sanchin	Breathing exercises.
seiryoku zenryo	Maximum efficiency with minimum effort.
seishi o choetsu	A state "beyond life and death."
seiza	Sitting-kneeling position.
seppuku	Honorable death of suicide; also called *hara-kiri.*
shikake-waza	Offensive attack techniques.
shin	Mind, heart.

shinjin	"The real you," the true person.
shinjutsu	"The skills of the mind and heart."
sho	Captain.
shogun	Samurai monarch.
shuchu-ryoku	Concentration of all one's power on one point.
sodo	Spearsmanship. The Way of the spear.
sohei	Well-trained warrior monks.
sono-mama	Things as they really are, "suchness."
Sonshi	Japanese translation of the name Sun Tzu, a Chinese military theorist highly regarded by the samurai.
suki	A gap of space between objects; in warriorship, an opening that can be taken advantage of.
suki o mitsukeru	To take advantage of an opening *(suki)* in the opponent's defense.
tai no sen	Counterattack.
tai ten	Also *tanden, tan-tien, seika tanden;* the one point; the body's center of gravity, two inches below the navel.
taiken	"Body knowledge."
Taira	Family of warriors; enemies of the Minamoto.
taisho	General.
Taoism	A Chinese philosophy of living.
teppo	Firearms.
tessendo	Use of the war fan *(tessen)*.
Tokimune	A regent of the Hojo family (1251–84).
tomaranu kokoro	"A mind that knows no stopping."
tomaru	Stopping, abiding.
toraware	"Caught."
uchi-ne	The art of throwing arrows.
uchiotoshi-waza	Striking down an opponent when he is out of balance.
uji	Clan.
ushin	"The mind conscious of itself."
waza	Striking technique.
yaburu	Fighter who lacks perfected technique but possesses spirit and courage.
yotsu te o hanasu	"To release four hands."
yugamae	Bow-holding posture.
zan-totsu	"Close and strike," the tactics of the samurai.
zanshin	"Remaining mind."
Zen	A Japanese form of Chinese Ch'an Buddhism; "the religion of the samurai."